To Jan —
Walk with Jesus!
Pastor Dan

Foreword by John Ashcroft

Jesus and You

25 ways to grow your life in Christ

Compiled and Edited by

George O. Wood
Hal Donaldson
Ken Horn

Jesus and You
25 ways to grow your life in Christ
Compiled and Edited by George O. Wood, Hal Donaldson, and Ken Horn

Printed in the United States of America
ISBN: 1-880689-15-4
Copyright 2006, Onward Books, Inc.

Cover design by KeyArt

The opinions contained herein do not necessarily represent the views of other participants.

Scripture quotations marked *NIV* are taken from the *New International Version*. Copyright 1973, 1978, 1984, International Bible Society. Scripture quotations marked *NKJV* are taken from the *New King James Version*. Copyright 1979, 1980, 1982, Thomas Nelson, Inc. Publishers. Scripture quotations marked *KJV* are from the *King James Version* of the Bible. Scripture quotations marked *Amplified* are taken from the *Amplified Bible*. Copyright 1987, The Lockman Foundation. Scripture quotations marked *TLB* are taken from the *The Living Bible*. Copyright 1971, Tyndale House Publishers. Scripture quotations marked *NLT* are taken from the *New Living Translation*. Copyright 1996, Tyndale House Publishers. Scripture quotations marked *The Message* are taken from the *The Message*. Copyright 2002, Navpress. Scripture references with no version noted are from the last noted version.

To Jewel, my faithful wife of 40 years.

George O. Wood

To my wife, Doree, who believes God for the impossible.

Hal Donaldson

To Peggy, the love of my life. You have stood beside me in good times and hard times.

Ken Horn

CONTENTS

SECTION THREE:
LIVING WITH DIRECTION

SECTION FOUR:
LIVING WITH PURPOSE

SECTION FIVE:
LIVING WITH POWER

FOREWORD

My friendship with George Wood goes back to the days when we were teenagers in the youth group at our home church in Springfield, Missouri. When George asked me to write the foreword to this book, I accepted if my endorsement would accomplish two things: (1) be an encouragement to others to receive the practical help for Christian living contained in this book, and (2) advance the cause of humanitarian assistance to those in need—in view of the fact the proceeds from this book are going to the great cause of Convoy of Hope.

Thus, I am happy to recommend this book to you. It's written by 25 men and women, all of them in ministry of one kind or another, who know firsthand some of the practical dimensions of Christian living. Thus, the title: *Jesus and You: 25 ways to grow your life in Christ*.

I invite you to take a journey of discovery through the ways Jesus can grow your life, and the ways you can draw closer to Him. The authors who penned these chapters minister these truths as their way of life. But they learned them the same way you will, by their own personal relationship with Jesus. These chapters won't do the work for you, but they will help point the way.

Several years ago, I listened as George Wood presented the material found in the first chapter of this book—"Developing His Character Within You." It's a fresh way of looking at a passage we know as The Beatitudes, and I found it most insightful. His first chapter sets the tone for everything that follows. Read it, and then in the succeeding chapters choose the topics that speak most to your life right now.

One of the key themes in my own life has been the passage from Deuteronomy 30, which deals with the responsibility each of us has to choose life or death. Choice is the great freedom given to us by our Creator and Redeemer. My desire for you is that you will always make the kind of choices that advance God's purposes for you; and that your choices will result in not only a better life for yourself, but also for your family, community, and the world at large. It is my desire that the chapters in this book help you make those better kinds of choices—choices that will assist you in your personal growth and deepen your relationship with Jesus Christ.

John Ashcroft
Former Attorney General of the United States

ACKNOWLEDGMENTS

Special thanks to Peggy Horn, Scott Harrup,
and Matt Key.

Section 7

"*The starting place for all spiritual, personal, relational, and emotional growth is poverty—the recognition that we need help.*"

—George O. Wood

Character	George O. Wood
Confidence	Thomas Lindberg
Joy	Russell W. Eggert
Temptation	Dan Secrist
Humility	Leigh Metcalf

CHAPTER 1

Developing His Character Within You

GEORGE O. WOOD

Just a few months after I became pastor of a then small and struggling church, Dr. Robert Frost, a leader in the charismatic renewal movement, prayed for me and the church: "Lord, help them to build foundations strong enough to bear the weight You will later place on them."

That's what Jesus seeks to do for us by giving a teaching in the Sermon on the Mount that we identify as the Beatitudes (Matthew 5:1-12). The eight qualities form the bedrock foundation for a life well built. The principles arise out of Jesus' own character, and when we put them into operation we fulfill the biblical desire that Christ be formed in us (Galatians 4:19).

Rather than looking at these character foundations from old English, see them through the lens of self-affirmations. Jesus wants you to be able to say the following things about yourself—because when you live these statements, you are expressing the personality of our Lord.

I NEED HELP

The first Beatitude pronounces blessing on the poor in spirit.

There are two kinds of poverty: that of a student or minimum-wage worker just barely getting by, and that of a person so destitute he or she is totally dependent on others for food, shelter, and clothing.

It's that second kind of poverty that Jesus refers to here—the destitute in spirit, a poverty never relieved by our own efforts.

Jesus tells us that we must live with an attitude that says, "I need help." The Christian life begins when we say, "Lord, I cannot buy salvation, forgiveness, or eternal life. I am totally dependent on You for what I cannot give myself." That attitude of "I need help" is meant to mark us for the length of our Christian journey. Look at how upset the Lord was with the Laodicean church when they forgot about the need to be poor in spirit (Revelation 3:17).

Jesus modeled this principle for us in the Garden of Gethsemane when He told Peter, James, and John to watch and pray with Him because His soul was "overwhelmed with sorrow" (Matthew 26:38, NIV). What if the Lord had taken the attitude "I don't need help. I'm the Son of God. Why should I tell these three disciples that I need them with Me? I cannot let them hear that I'm sad; they will lose confidence in Me."

But Jesus was honest about His feelings and plainly expressed to those closest to Him that He needed their help.

The starting place for all spiritual, personal, relational, and emotional growth is poverty—the recognition that we need help. Jesus said, "Apart from me you can do nothing" (John 15:5). The "I need help" people get the Kingdom (Matthew 5:3).

I AM SENSITIVE

The shortest verse in the Bible records, "Jesus wept" (John 11:35). He could have maintained a clinical detachment over the death of His friend Lazarus. But Jesus never got calloused or professional in dealing with the needs and hurts of others. He remained sensitive.

Thus, the Lord gives blessing to those who mourn (Matthew 5:4). We must be persons easily moved by the hurts that we have done or that others have had done to them. The hard-hearted never know the comfort of the Lord.

I AM STRONG, BUT EASY TO LIVE WITH

The word *meek* has gotten bad press. We think of meek as weak, timid, spineless—a person who is a doormat spread out for others to walk on. But when Jesus says the meek are blessed, He uses a word that means three things: (1) a centered or balanced person, (2) an individual under restraint or control, and (3) a man or woman of gentleness.

The word *meek* in Greek literature was used to describe a wild horse that was broken. It still had verve, power, and speed—but its energies had been channeled.

Jesus wants you to be a person not given to erratic behavior or mood swings. He wants you balanced—not all work and not all play. He desires you to be gentle—notice how gentle He was even with little children. He also desires you to be disciplined—not living your life in chaos, but seeking to bring order, purpose, clarity, and priority to your life.

No wonder the meek inherit the earth—they know how to run their own life, their family and work, and their world.

I WANT TO KEEP ON GROWING

Jesus blessed those who hunger and thirst after righteousness. There is never a time when we can say, "I have arrived. I know it all." Nor can we ever say, "I have become totally like Christ."

We must stay on the growing edge.

There are five great growth lists in the New Testament: the

eight Beatitudes (Matthew 5:1-12), the 22 life responses of Romans 12:9-21, the 15 qualities of love in 1 Corinthians 13:4-8, the nine fruit of the Spirit in Galatians 5:22,23, and the seven "add-ons" to faith in 1 Peter 1:5-9. In all, 61 qualities from all five lists. These traits define what it is to live a righteous life. If you hunger and thirst after being this kind of person, you will be—as Jesus promised—satisfied!

I CARE

The Beatitudes are much like the locks on the Panama Canal. The Atlantic and Pacific oceans are not at the same level. In order to move ships from one ocean to the other, engineers could not simply dig a channel and let the water run through. Instead, they had to devise an integrated system of large locks that lowered or raised the water so that ships could pass through in stages.

Notice the sequence in Jesus' teaching. At the beginning you are not able to give help since you need help. So, the first Beatitude is about being poor in spirit. But as you develop the attitude of dependence upon the Lord, and as you become sensitive, strong but easy to live with, and grow in your Christian walk—transformation takes place. Now you are in a position to give help. You are ready for the fifth Beatitude.

The "I care" person possesses a quality in mercy that keeps one away from a spirit of harshness, coldness, judgmentalism, and criticism. The "I care" man or woman chooses, like the Good Samaritan, to move out of their own concerns and duties into the hurts and needs of others. Mother Teresa wonderfully lived this quality and expressed it through this prayer: "Let every action of mine be something beautiful for God."

MY CONSCIENCE IS CLEAR

How do you get a pure heart?
When I was a little boy in northwest China, the son of mis-

sionary parents, we had no running water. I only had to take a bath once a week. I'm embarrassed now to admit it, but my goal every Saturday night was to make the ring around the tub thicker than any previously! My mother practically had to use a Brillo pad to clean my ears!

I never let the grime build up now because I am an adult who showers daily.

Sometimes sin and unforgiveness build up in our lives much like I used to let the dirt accumulate on me. How do we get clean?

Old King David, the adulterer and murderer, tells us in Psalm 32 how to clear your conscience when you have done wrong—through confession and repentance. It would be wonderful if for the rest of your life you never had a wrong thought or action. But we know that's not the case. We must continually confess to the Lord the things we did that we ought not to have done, and the things we did not do that we ought (1 John 1:8,9).

The tear duct gland is to the eye what repentance and confession are to the heart—they wash away impurities.

LET ME BE YOUR FRIEND

The seventh Beatitude gives a blessing to peacemakers.

It's much easier to blow up a bridge than to build one. Jesus asks us to be bridge-builders in two ways: Everyone needs to make peace with God and with others. Therefore, the peacemaker is both evangelist (bringing others to Jesus) and healer (working to bring reconciliation in family, among friends, and throughout society).

At many times in his ministry, Billy Graham has been criticized for reaching out to include people that some have wanted to exclude. He has responded on occasion by quoting this poem:

He drew a circle that shut me out,
Rebel, heretic, a thing to flout.
But love and I had the wit to win.
We drew a circle that took him in.

When you have the attitude "Let me be your friend," God calls you His son. Why? Because even God's one and only Son was called the friend of sinners (Matthew 11:19). "He came and preached peace to you who were far away and peace to those who were near" (Ephesians 2:17).

I WILL REJOICE, EVEN IN MY DOWN TIMES

The last Beatitude is the hardest one to master, and that's why it's last in the list: "Blessed are those who are persecuted . . . . Rejoice, and be glad . . ." (Matthew 5:10-12).

When you develop the first seven Beatitudes as integral to your personality, then the end result is a lifestyle shaped by Jesus himself. You will stand out. And there will be people who oppose what you now represent.

Whether our down times come as a result of outside opposition or tough circumstances, the Scriptures consistently tell us to rejoice. Writing from a prison cell, Paul tells believers, "Rejoice in the Lord always. I will say it again: Rejoice!" (Philippians 4:4). Paul encourages us to "rejoice in our sufferings, because we know that suffering produces perseverance; perseverance, character; and character, hope" (Romans 5:3,4). James reminds us, "Consider it pure joy, my brothers, whenever you face trials of many kinds" (James 1:2).

Rejoice in trials, tests, and trouble? Yes! Exactly!

We are being asked to respond reflectively rather than reflexively to difficulties. What's the difference?

When I go to the doctor for my physical exam, he taps me on the knee with an instrument that looks like a hammer. My lower leg immediately kicks out—something called a "knee-jerk" reaction.

Jesus tells us not to have the reflexive "knee-jerk" reaction to life's adversities, but instead to put a space between the action against us and our reaction. That space is for reflection—and the desired reflection is an attitude of joy.

Like I said, this is the hardest Beatitude to learn! But, we can have joy because we know instantly the end result. The adversity, suffering, or persecution is never the end of the story—it's only the beginning. We see beyond the difficulty to the ultimate joy of God working out everything for good to those who love Him and are called according to His purpose (Romans 8:28).

FROM MIRACLE TO MATURITY

Have you noticed the segment of Gospel that immediately precedes Jesus' teaching on the Beatitudes? Look at the last few verses of Matthew 4. They record the wide sweep of Jesus' healing and deliverance power, as well as the huge throngs from all places that crowded around Him.

If I were with Jesus at that moment in time, I would have urged Him to continue His ministry of miracles. Breaking away from that to teach risked losing the crowds and the momentum. But Jesus knows human nature better than His disciples or I. His miracles only change people's external circumstances, but not their internal disposition of heart.

We must be careful that we not get so focused on Jesus doing something *for* us that we forget He wants to do something *in* us.

The eight attitudes of the Beatitudes instill into our minds and hearts the very personality of Jesus. When you pray to be like Jesus, tell yourself that He desires you to say these things truthfully about yourself:

- I need help.
- I am sensitive.
- I am strong, but easy to live with.
- I want to keep on growing.
- I care.

- My conscience is clear.
- Let me be your friend.
- I will rejoice, even in my down times.

For the author's biographical information, see "About the Editors" on page 237.

CHAPTER 2

Confidence for Living

THOMAS LINDBERG

Most people have heard of the famous leaning Tower of Pisa. It leans nearly 20 feet out of perpendicular, and several experts are fearful that it is in danger of falling. How did the tower get into such a predicament? The original architect drew plans for a 170-foot-high structure on a 10-foot foundation. No wonder the tower leans. It's a tall building with a small foundation.

I suspect there are many people who attend church Sunday after Sunday who have a "leaning Tower of Pisa" life. The pressures of life have taken their toll, and now these folks are beginning to lean. There are even some (perhaps some of you who read these words) like the tower in Italy who are in danger of falling or collapsing.

No one needs to convince you that life today can be difficult, and at times downright demanding. Just read the paper or listen to the news. Or live through a month of job pressure, family problems, health difficulties, or financial stresses, and you'll have no trouble believing that life can be rough and intimidating.

How can a person live with confidence amid all those pressures? There is an answer. Walk closely to Jesus. I've discovered in my years of Christian living, but even more importantly, through my careful study of God's Word, that the person who walks closely to Jesus can experience confidence for living each day.

Do you realize that as a believer in the Lord Jesus Christ, you have an insurance policy with God that will supply confidence for living? This policy takes force the moment you are born again by repentance toward God and faith in Christ. The policy is free (see Isaiah 55:1) and it contains no pre-existing conditions (see 1 John 3:1,2). Let me show you your policy with God. You can read the coverage in Romans 8:28: "We know that all things work together for good to those who love God, to those who are the called according to His purpose" (NKJV). Together, let's leaf through the inspired words of your policy with God so that you can walk closely to Jesus and develop confidence in life.

YOU HAVE A UNIVERSAL PLAN

The verse begins by emphasizing "all things." Romans 8 starts with "no condemnation" and ends with "no separation." Then right in the middle of the chapter, verse 28 says that God works "all things" together for our good. That is what I call a universal plan. Not long ago I had lunch with an agnostic. He told me, "I'm not sure God even exists. But if He does, He sure doesn't care a hoot about people." Thank God that man's wrong! God cares so much for you that He is working "all things" together for you.

Jesus said that when a sparrow falls to the ground, God knows all about it (Matthew 10:29). The Bible teaches that God knows our needs before we ask (Matthew 6:8). And God tells us that He knows the clear plan He has for our lives (Jeremiah 29:11). Read those three verses carefully (and dozens more could be added) and you'll see one dominant theme: God knows all things about us.

How can God take *all things*—even past failures, present faults, and future fears—and work them for good? Well, think of a cook. A good cook can take baking soda, baking powder, salt, flour, and other ingredients that are not tasty by themselves, mix them all together, and end up with a delicious chocolate cake. If a cook can do that with distasteful ingredients, how much more God is able to take *all things* and bring forth good. Knowing that increases confidence in life.

YOU HAVE AN ENERGETIC PLAN

In Romans 8:28, the Holy Spirit inspired the verb "work" to be in your Bible. The Greek word implies intense, hard, tireless work. It's used of a workman carving out a road. That's work! God is tirelessly working to blend all things for good in your life. As Psalm 121:4 says, "Indeed, he who watches over Israel never slumbers or sleeps" (NLT).

There are some powerful verses in Proverbs that remind followers of Jesus that God is always working on their behalf.

- "Commit your actions to the Lord, and your plans will succeed" (16:3).
- "We can make our plans, but the Lord determines our steps" (16:9).
- "You can make many plans, but the Lord's purpose will prevail" (19:21).

You see, even as you read those words, God is working in you and for you. Just think of that fact! That will give you confidence for living.

Think with me of the day Jesus was hammered to the cross. His disciples scattered like leaves in a strong wind. The earth shook. The sky turned black as ink. The devils in hell shouted with glee, "He's dead!" Everything looked black. But God was working. Three days later Jesus was raised from the dead and the Savior was back in business, mightier than ever. May I remind you that the same God is actively working in your life.

Some may scoff and sneer, calling that kind of thinking "pie-in-the-sky." Romans 8:37 calls it being "more than conquerors through Him who loved us" (NKJV). I'll stand by inspired Saint Paul rather than uninspired Mr. Scoffer any day. Take hope, my friend! God has a working, energetic plan for your life. Let confidence in God's power fill you daily as you walk with Him.

YOU HAVE A BENEFICIAL PLAN

Our verse teaches us that God is working all things together for our good. That's what I call a beneficial plan. Some of you may be asking, "If God's in charge and working all things for good, why do Christians face disease, divorce, difficulties, distress, depression, and death?" God caused none of those things to ultimately harm us. We live in a sin-soaked world that reels from its consequences. Yes, one day there will be no more disease, divorce, difficulties, distress, depression, or death. But until that day, here's the big truth we need to catch and etch on our hearts: With God's help we can see pain turned to gain, scars turned to stars, and miseries turned to miracles. How is that possible? Because God works all things together for good.

For example, Joseph spent about 17 years in an Egyptian jail. Years later he looked back on that experience and revealed, "As far as I'm concerned, God turned into good what you meant for evil" (Genesis 50:20, NLT). Or, consider Paul the apostle. He's locked away in a Roman prison. What's his perspective? Philippians 1:12 records, "I want you to know that everything that has happened to me here has helped to spread the Good News." Both Joseph and Paul lived with confidence in God and believed that the Lord could bring good out of any situation.

One of the greatest preachers America ever produced was Jonathan Edwards. His preaching helped bring sweeping revival to New England during the 1730s. At the young age of 54, he suddenly died. His godly wife, Sarah, wrote this letter to their daughter two weeks after her father's death:

"My dearest daughter, what shall I say? A holy and good God has covered us with a dark cloud. Oh, that we may kiss the rod and lay our hands over our mouths. The Lord has done it. But my God still lives, and He has my heart. Oh, what a legacy my husband and your father has left us. We are fully given over to God."

Sarah Edwards believed her life was in God's hand. Do you? When you do, you will pray and believe God for miracles, and you will also have faith that His will is being worked out in your life for your good.

Colossians 3:3 teaches that "your life is hidden with Christ in God" (NKJV). Think of that—hidden in God! Let me illustrate the implications of that. Imagine you have a book and a small piece of paper. You open the book, slip the paper inside, and then shut the book. No one is able to lay a finger on that paper without first touching the book, right?

Now, let the book represent Jesus and let the paper represent you. The Bible says that your life is hidden in Christ. That means no one nor anything can touch your life without first going through the loving, caring hand of Jesus. That ought to give you confidence in life. There aren't any events that intersect our lives that can fool God or catch Him by surprise.

YOU HAVE A SPECIFIC PLAN

For whom did God design this plan? Any Tom, Dick, or Harry? No, our verse says God's insurance policy is for "those who love God." Have you given your life to Christ and asked Him to save you? Have you acknowledged you cannot save yourself and sought Christ to become your Savior? You're the person for whom God designed this amazing plan.

My Uncle Marvin was a great gardener. One summer while visiting with him, I spotted the most perfect apple on one of his trees. As I walked closer to admire this beauty, I discovered it was a wooden apple, perfectly shaped, painted, and then hung like a Christmas ornament on the tree. "What's this?" I exclaimed.

My uncle responded, "The bugs think it's a real apple. They land on it and leave my real apples alone. That wooden apple fools the bugs."

Let me be clear: No one can fool the Lord about their love for Him. Second Timothy 2:19 teaches us, "The Lord knows those who are His." He reads you like a book. Today, if you've never asked Jesus Christ to save you, let me urge you to do so. Pray to God, call a friend, or talk with a pastor. Nothing in life will bring greater confidence, joy, and freedom than to know God will sovereignly work everything in your life for good.

YOU HAVE A CERTAIN PLAN

The New Testament was originally written in Greek. In Greek grammar, the words that start a sentence are often the ones the writer wanted to emphasize, the ones that assert his main idea. The first words of Romans 8:28 are "we know." The Bible is saying that God's universal, energetic, beneficial, specific plan is more than a hope or a hunch; it's a certain fact.

When our daughter was born, I recall bringing her home from the hospital. When it was time for her to go to sleep at night, we would lay her in her crib and close the door. She would cry and cry. As I stood just outside her door, I thought, *Amy, don't be afraid and cry. If you only knew that your mom and I are just outside your room. We love you. We will provide for you. We have plans for you. I know you don't understand all this, but your life is in our hands and you can trust us.*

That's what God is saying to you and me today.

Dr. Thomas Lindberg is senior pastor of the 2,500-member First Assembly of God of Memphis in Cordova, Tennessee. He has earned a master of theology degree from Gordon-Conwell Theological Seminary (Boston) and the doctor of ministry degree from Luther Rice Seminary (Atlanta). He has contributed chapters to several books and has authored more than 150 articles for various journals and magazines.

Lindberg has served as a pastor in the Assemblies of God since 1976. He has been elected to several district council positions, has spoken at many statewide conferences as well as being the keynote speaker for district councils. He currently serves as a director of Evangel University and the World

Missions Board. He and his wife, Sandi, live in Memphis and have two sons and a daughter. You may reach him at tlindberg@firstassemblymemphis.org.

CHAPTER 3

Abundant Joy

RUSSELL W. EGGERT

"Our mouths were filled with laughter, our tongues with songs of joy" (Psalm 126:2, NIV).

The Israelites went through numerous highs and lows throughout their history. One of the more joyous occasions was when they returned to Jerusalem from captivity. Psalm 126 speaks of the excitement and joy they were experiencing. It states they were like men in a dream, or awakened from one that seemed too good to be true. Imagine the excitement of returning home after decades had passed. The promise of God had always been that His people would return to the Promised Land, but it just seemed too good to even imagine. Now the time had come and their hearts overflowed with laughter and songs of joy.

When I close my eyes and imagine this picture, it is not a typical worship service in a synagogue or church that comes to mind. It is more like a celebration in an Irish pub or college frat house. Are you surprised? But I'm not talking about drunkenness. I'm talking about a room filled with joyous laughter and boisterous songs. So often, such joy seems distant from our sober, dignified, solemn worship services where even a giggle would seem out of place.

COMMANDED TO REJOICE

In this verse, we read of people reveling in the good news of God. They were rejoicing that the impossible had indeed become reality—they were back home. I can imagine an older man dancing as his heart overflows with joyous excitement at seeing the city of Jerusalem. Just recently in a public marketplace, God answered a prayer for me and I got "happy feet" for about three seconds. One believer next to me almost had a stroke and another one talked about it for days. Evidently, if a Christian is smitten with a sudden feeling of abundant joy, moving your feet quickly is unacceptable, unless you are in a sanctuary with the proper music being played and there are sufficient witnesses to testify that the occurrence was inspired by the Holy Spirit. My problem was my heart told my feet to "get happy" before my brain could say, "Not here!"

As I read through Scripture, I am amazed at how often joy is mentioned. It seems clear to me that God desires us—no, *commands* us—to rejoice. In the Old Testament, we read that God wanted His people to be obedient to Him so that He could supply them with abundance. He wanted to give them a "land of milk and honey," a place of wine and song. They were to sing of His goodness (Exodus 15), play tambourines and dance (Exodus 15:20) at God's exploits, and rejoice in their Maker (Psalm 149:2). Israel had a history of rejoicing in the victories God gave them over their enemies (2 Chronicles 20:27). We read about the Feast of Tabernacles, how the Israelites were to "rejoice before the Lord [their] God for seven days. Celebrate this as a festival to the Lord for seven days each year" (Leviticus 23:40,41). Words like *feast, festival,* and *celebrate* are all words of joy.

Why does God want His people to rejoice? He wants His people to express abundant joy because we are a reflection of Him. God is a God of joy. How can I be so sure of this? One of the fruits of the Holy Spirit is joy (Galatians 5:22), and the Holy Spirit is God. Another reason we see God as joyful is in

His response to creation. What did God say about creation? From day two on, "God saw that it was good." How do you respond when you do or see something good? The natural reaction is to smile. When we see "good" it brings joy to our heart. At the end of the sixth day, "God saw all that he had made, and it was very good" (Genesis 1:31).

OUR SOURCE OF JOY

Joy is vital in the life of the believer. It flows from our relationship with Jesus Christ. Just as we receive joy from the love given to us by others, that joy is compounded when we realize how much God loves us. When you express your love to others, it gives you joy. That also becomes multiplied when we understand how much God loves to hear our voices express praise and adoration to Him. Joy is a source of strength. Nehemiah exhorted the Israelites to "enjoy choice food and sweet drinks, and send some to those who have nothing prepared. This day is sacred to our Lord. Do not grieve, for the joy of the Lord is your strength" (Nehemiah 8:10). Most of us realize that problems look smaller, the sun shines brighter, and everything is hopeful when we have joy. Joy is the flowers in a garden. Joy is the cool breeze on a warm summer day. Joy is cool mountain water. Joy is refreshing, invigorating, and energizing.

We must remind ourselves that joy is different from happiness. Happiness is dependent on circumstances, while joy is a positive, at times euphoric, feeling even when circumstances are negative. What then is the source of this joy spoken of in the Bible? It is none other than God himself. Psalm 43:4 says, "Then will I go to the altar of God, to God, my joy and my delight."

The Book of Nehemiah is all about the construction of the wall of Jerusalem. Israelites had been allowed to return from captivity to build the wall. At first the task appeared immense and too difficult for the people of the city. God used Nehemiah to inspire the people to believe that God could give them strength and protect them as they worked on the wall. When the wall was completed, two choirs proceeded in opposite directions around the wall giving thanks to God. "And on that day they offered great sacrifices, rejoicing because God had given them great joy. The women and the children also rejoiced. The sound of rejoicing in Jerusalem could be heard far away" (Nehemiah 12:43).

All through the Psalms and the prophetic books the message of rejoicing remains the same. The people were not called upon to rejoice because they had just any god; they responded with joy because they had *the* God. The God who cared about them, provided for them, protected them, and was jealous of their love. He wanted to be their source of joy.

Habakkuk 3:17,18 says it well: "Though the fig tree does not bud and there are no grapes on the vines, though the olive crop fails and the fields produce no food, though there are no sheep in the pen and no cattle in the stalls, yet I will rejoice in the Lord, I will be joyful in God my Savior." How can you make this statement unless you have great faith in God to do the miraculous? When we trust in God, there is an anticipatory joy as we wait to see what God will do. It is when there are impossibilities that He gets to demonstrate His divine power.

Jesus taught that God desires the believer to have abundant life (John 10:10). The announcement of the birth of Jesus was a message of great joy (Luke 2:10). Jesus told His disciples that part of God's plan is to make our joy complete (John 15:11; 16:24). The life of the follower of Christ is to reflect that joy that God gives.

The excitement of the Resurrection was continued in the Early Church. The promise of the Father occurred on the Day of Pentecost. The 120 believers began speaking in other tongues and a large crowd gathered. Since some in the crowd made fun of the believers and accused them of being drunk, we can safely assume that they exhibited some behaviors associated with drunkenness, like excessive joy. In Acts 3 there is the story of the beggar at the temple gate who was healed. He displayed abundant joy. He leaped to his feet, walked, and jumped, praising God. His antics attracted a large crowd, giving Peter an opportunity to preach again. When the gospel came to Samaria with power to heal and deliver, the whole city was filled with great joy. There were many struggles for the infant church and its apostles. There were times of persecution, famine in the land of Israel, and hostile reception from governments and religious groups, but the current of abundant joy runs through the Book of Acts like a river through a valley.

CHOOSING JOY

How can we participate in this abundant joy? We must put our trust and confidence in Jesus. He is the One who will watch over us in every way. Despite our present circumstances, we know God will take care of our every need. Joy comes from knowing it doesn't depend on me, whatever the "it" is. Joy comes from knowing God loves me even when I am unlovable. Joy comes from knowing He wants my love. He treasures it.

I am sure many of you have love notes written to you by a parent, a child, or "that special someone." We keep the special ones to read over and over because they bring so much joy to us. But there is something even better and that is when you find a note that you wrote in the past that is being kept as a treasure. Your heart overflows with joy. In a similar way, God keeps your prayers, your "love notes" to Him (Revelation 5:8).

The first fruit of the Spirit of God listed in Galatians 5:22,23 is love. God is love, so it is easy for us to understand the importance of displaying love. The second fruit is joy. Joy comes before peace, patience, kindness, goodness, faithfulness, gentleness, and self-control. We know that we should have all of the fruits, but joy is given special emphasis. Jesus wants us to have abundant life and also to be appealing to a world full of sadness, doubt, and hopelessness.

I met a man who came bouncing across the parking lot shouting, "I have just been fired!"

My response was, "Are you going to be all right?"

He answered with a large smile, "Yes, God must have something very special, because this was a job I liked." God did have something very special that he would have missed if employed. Joy in the midst of difficulty is possible when we trust in God.

What brings you joy? Is it looking at someone or something beautiful? Is your joy in knowing you are loved? God has made us able to experience joy in so many ways.

When was the last time you had "happy feet"? Was it when you found a special sale on a dress or pair of shoes you've been wanting? Was it when your wife made your favorite meal? Was it when your granddaughter scored the winning goal? Was it when you heard a new song in church and began to tap your foot to the rhythm of the music (much to the shock of your spouse)? Whatever its cause, knowing Jesus Christ makes that joy more abundant. Thank God for the joy He brings, and determine to share it with others.

Dr. Russell W. Eggert has master's degrees in biblical literature and educational administration. He received a doctor of ministries degree from Trinity University in Deerfield, Illinois. He has been in ministry with the Assemblies of God for 35 years, much of this time in cross-cultural fields. He and his family have lived in Cape Town, South Africa, where he taught at Cape College of Theology and worked with people of Islamic and Hindu backgrounds. He is presently on the Board of Trustees for Valley Forge Christian College and continues to do ministry overseas. He is married to Carol and has three children and six grandchildren.

CHAPTER 4

When Temptation Comes

DAN SECRIST

"But each one is tempted when, by his own evil desire, he is dragged away and enticed. Then, after desire has conceived, it gives birth to sin; and sin, when it is full-grown, gives birth to death" (James 1:14,15, NIV).

What is so mysterious about temptation? Why can't we just "make a decision" not to indulge? Why do prominent spiritual leaders suddenly fall into egregious sin and thereby shame not only themselves, but also the very causes they proclaim?

I would love to call this chapter "How to Permanently Defeat Temptation," but that would be misleading. Battles with temptation are guaranteed in this fallen world and Jesus was the only one who managed to win every battle. "For all have sinned and fall short of the glory of God" (Romans 3:23). I don't have to define it or explain it. When you are invited to violate your beliefs, values, or goals, you have a conflict within. That's temptation. And we all lose some of these attacks that come against our souls.

While I have not always been successful in resisting temptation, I certainly have a lot of experience in dealing with it! Remember the old joke? "Lead me not into temptation; I can find the way myself." It's all too easy.

CARELESS SIN

One type of temptation leads to the slip-up along the way, the mistake of judgment, the careless decision, the sudden rise of anger. While these intrusive sins cause us remorse and pain, they are like stones along the trail that may cause us to stumble. We've simply not been paying attention. They don't usually cause us to lose the way or collapse. We turn to Jesus, repent, kick them aside, and move forward.

BESETTING SIN

The real challenges to our faith are the addictions, the habits, the temptations we face over and over that entice and discourage us. In the King James Version they are described as "besetting sins." We either learn to overcome them or we surrender, accept them, and live with them.

When I was a child, my mother once went to her sewing box, removed a spool of thread, and tied a single strand around my arms pinning them against my body. Then she said, "See if you can break it."

I pushed out my elbows and easily snapped the thread. Then she repeated the procedure using two wraps of thread. I easily broke them. As the game continued and she circled my body with more and more thread it finally became impossible to break free.

"Sin is like that," she said. "It may not seem hard to overcome one failure, but if you keep doing that sin you will be bound and unable to escape."

Temptation always comes with an offer. The hook is always baited and made attractive. Ironically, we know that. We even see the hook in the bait, but the bait looks so attractive that we simply ignore the hook and indulge in the pleasure of the bait. Soon enough comes the pain of regret, the sorrow of guilt, and the soul is degraded a little bit more.

When you are at that hurting moment, that lonely moment, that angry moment, that frustrated moment, the bait is dropped in front of you. Unless you have fortified your soul in advance, you will take the bait even though you know it will ultimately cause you pain. Your weakness may be sex, food, drugs, anger, pornography, alcohol, or even some legitimate hobby that you overindulge. But the enemy of your soul whispers, *You deserve some of that pleasure and you deserve it now. Forget the future! This is going to feel good.*

And it often does feel good . . . at least until you are finished. There is pleasure in sin for a season (Hebrews 11:25). If there weren't some initial gratification, who would indulge? But then comes the guilt, the remorse, the self-hatred, the "I did it again."

Tragically, our whole culture encourages indulgence rather than discipline. In fact, self-restraint, a crucial gift that Christianity brought to Western civilization, has now been largely replaced with self-esteem—which is quickly on its way to being replaced with self-indulgence.

BUILDING SOUL STRUCTURE

If you want your body to be healthy, you need to eat right, exercise, rest, and avoid unhealthy activities. Your body will fight off germs and disease much easier. The same goes for your soul. If you want to live victoriously, you must care for your soul on a regular basis. If you wait until a temptation hits and you are not spiritually fit, you're going to get hooked.

We seek to make the body comfortable. Overcoming temptation is learning to make the spirit comfortable. When you are at peace with God, you are at peace with yourself and far less likely to betray your values by sinning against them.

I read of a monk in the Middle Ages who, when tempted with sexual thoughts, was so horrified that he stripped and ran naked through a briar patch. Gasping for air, bleeding and wounded, his temptation passed. It might have worked for him, but it's probably not the best technique for winning a battle over temptation!

I remember Winkey Pratney saying, "The devil laughs at our

notebooks full of unapplied truth." It's not for lack of information that we sin, it's the lack of formation. Reading all the books in the world about temptation will not keep you from having an affair or getting addicted to drugs or being lazy. It is the application of the truth that liberates.

A young Christian preparing his or her income taxes may say, "I shouldn't cheat because God won't like it." A growing Christian would say, "This is not what God would have me do." A mature Christian says, "That's not who I am." The character is formed. In computer parlance, holiness is trained into our lives until we change the labels and the default. We start with Jesus as part of the "pull-down menu," but Christian maturity makes Him the default in our lives.

DEVELOPING THE DEFAULT

Bible reading and prayer, followed by worship, meditation, and fellowship are near the top of everyone's list. But following a list is not the answer. If you approach Christian maturity as God's call on your life and begin training for it, temptation's hook is far less likely to puncture your soul. The healthiest way to understand this is, as John Ortberg says, "training rather than trying." You train before the race, not during the race. Here are some training exercises:

Confess your sins daily to the Lord. Exposing them to His light allows God to forgive and heal you. The longer you conceal and resist openness, the longer you are vulnerable to massive failures when temptations come. Allow the Lord into your life fully by confessing all your sins.

Draw close to Jesus. That sounds trite perhaps, but what I mean is to begin the day in spiritual preparation: prayer, meditation, reading the Bible and even devotional books. End the day with prayer before you get in bed. There was a season of overwhelming temptation in my life when I would simply kneel by my bed and pray the Lord's Prayer. I would especially emphasize, "Lead me not into temptation, but deliver me from evil." My life has been radically altered by this simple practice.

Time with Jesus not only steals time from flirting with your temptations, but that fellowship with Him fortifies your soul so that you might resist temptation. You only need to be born again one time, but you need to be saved from temptation every day, sometimes several times a day. And don't just pray *against* things, pray *toward* something. Focus your prayers on what you intend to *become*. Don't simply pray for help to *overcome*.

Fast, and discover spiritual strength. Typical Americans eat three meals a day and several snacks as well. I believe there is a key to conquering temptation hidden in the food right on your plate.

Jesus said, "When you fast . . . " (Matthew 6:17). He made the assumption that fasting is an integral part of discipleship, not an optional add-on. Then He gave specific instructions about fasting. Most of us do not find it easy to go without food, but I am convinced it is a powerful step to overcoming sin and temptation.

"But I tried fasting, and it doesn't work," you might say. "I get so hungry and then I eat even more at the next meal!"

You are not alone. Self-control is not easy, especially when it comes to eating. But start with just one meal. If that's too hard, start with giving up coffee, chocolate or sodas for a day. Begin to restrict in some degree what goes into your mouth. The fact it is difficult ought to be revealing. Every virtue has a price, and overcoming temptation is well worth the price.

Food is not the enemy, and fasting is not the total answer. But it is a powerful weapon Christians are encouraged to use.

Engage in Christian community. Jesus' directives cannot fully be lived out if you are not in a community of believers. Mature Christians are able to point out failures in a helpful way so you can make corrections and grow; and when you are making spiritual progress, you are less vulnerable to temptations. Belong to a local church and participate in a small group, too.

I have really come to believe that life change happens best in small groups, and regular fellowship in a healthy small group produces spiritual stamina. Will you continue to struggle with temptation alone, or will you take the step toward a healthier life by participating in Christian community? It takes effort, sometimes painful effort, but the reward is worth it.

Find times of solitude. I love time alone with God, but it's not easy to get away. How busy was Jesus? Yet He took time to get alone with the Father "very early in the morning" (Mark 1:35). Solitude gives the Holy Spirit time to develop your uniqueness. Do you realize what's at stake? Without solitude, a pastor may lose his anointing, an artist his creativity, a leader his humility, a businessman his energy.

In the process of building the character that fortifies you, you will still be tempted. Learn the antecedents to your behavior and avoid them. Don't walk into situations where temptations can easily grab you.

Finally, resisting temptation is more than spiritual disciplines. You need the presence of the Holy Spirit to save you. Defang the devil with James 4:7: "Submit yourselves, then, to God. Resist the devil, and he will flee from you." And the best weapon I know with which to resist the devil is to . . .

Speak in tongues. All the character development and prevention exercises are wonderful, but you are still going to face temptations. I believe the most powerful weapon given to us is speaking in tongues. At the moment of crisis, when the tempter is dangling that irresistible bait in front of you, pray in tongues. Tongues are far more than just the initial evidence of the Holy Spirit's fullness in a person's life.

On many occasions I have found myself attracted to some sin. If I call out to the Lord by praying in tongues, I am always amazed at how quickly the temptation passes. I don't have to pray for long, sometimes just a minute or two. By praying toward the Lord in tongues, I am focused on Him, not the temptation!

The battle against temptation is spiritual. All the disciplines are helpful, but I believe praying in tongues is our most powerful spiritual weapon in this perpetual battle.

Dan Secrist is the founding pastor of Faith Assembly of Lacey, Washington (www.faithassemblyoflacey.com). He is a graduate of Northwest University in Kirkland, Washington. During nine years as a missionary in Youth With A Mission he helped found ministries in Spain, Morocco, and Argentina. He preaches in fluent Spanish and has visited 80 countries to date. Currently he resides in Lacey with Susan, his wife of 29 years. They have two grown children, Justin and September. Personal hobbies include snow skiing in the winter and maintaining his Japanese garden in the summer.

CHAPTER 5

A Life That Honors God

LEIGH METCALF

Take a look at Genesis 1 and 2 and you are reminded of the wonderful plan God had for humanity when He created the world. Adam and Eve were created in God's image, and their lives were structured around God-given responsibilities.

Then sin came into the world and contaminated God's plan. Humanity needed to be redeemed from their sin. The sacrificial death of God's only Son was the only possible solution in restoring us to the relationship that He had intended. In essence, our character is flawed unless we reflect Christ's character.

God creates each of us to have specific strengths of character. He gives each one of us the ability to make decisions, to have the knowledge of God, and to have fellowship with Him. We, too, are created in God's image, even though this fallen world would disguise that fact. Through Christ, we are offered the chance to achieve the potential God desires for us.

But will we take that opportunity? Even after coming to Christ in faith, will we continue to grow into His image? Let's look at just two characteristics that we can nurture in our pursuit of a life that honors God.

INTEGRITY

Integrity is the core of our character. Integrity basically means wholeness or integration. It is the quality of bringing things together in harmony. From the believer's perspective, a life of integrity means outward actions and inner motivations are working together harmoniously in a manner pleasing to God.

Dis-integration pulls things apart. The life of sin calls on a person to disguise evil motivations and to hide immoral actions. Where integrity is the magnet that pulls life together, sin's disharmony creates brokenness at every turn.

The follower of Christ, then, responds to the Holy Spirit's conviction and roots out every sin that would begin to break down the wholeness God has created in his or her life. No part of the believer's life is held back from fellowship with and service to God.

"You shall love the Lord your God with all your heart, with all your soul, and with all your strength" (Deuteronomy 6:5, NKJV). Jesus quoted this as the greatest commandment in the law (Matthew 22:37). Every area of life must come under the lordship of Jesus. As you serve God with the wholeness of your life, then your mind, will, emotions, spirit, finances, marriage, and every other facet of your existence will be transformed.

When God's Word speaks of integrity, it connects it to blessing. In Psalm 7:8 we are told, "The Lord shall judge the peoples; judge me, O Lord, according to my righteousness, and according to my integrity within me." Do you want to face God's judgment of your life with faith and confidence? Live a life of integrity.

"Let integrity and uprightness preserve me, for I wait on You" (Psalm 25:21). Yes, even believers face sorrows and dangers in life, but they do not do so in a chaotic universe. When integrity and uprightness mark your life, you can come through life's trials as you wait on God in faith.

Integrity brings us into God's presence. "As for me, You

uphold me in my integrity, and set me before Your face forever" (Psalm 41:12).

"He who walks with integrity walks securely," Solomon tells us in Proverbs 10:9. Do you want your walk to be secured? There is no fear or doubt as you walk with God in integrity.

"Vindicate me, O Lord, for I have walked in my integrity. I have also trusted in the Lord; I shall not slip. Examine me, O Lord, and prove me; try my mind and my heart" (Psalm 26:1,2). Here we see a reminder of the source of our integrity. It is God who redeemed us through Christ. It is God who vindicates us, who preserves us, who through His divine scrutiny of our lives ever promotes His wholeness within us.

There's a beautiful picture of integrity in the Old Testament. We read that the high priest wore a pouch inside the breastplate over his heart (Exodus 28:30). In the pouch were two stones or sets of stones, Urim and Thummim, somehow used by the priest to determine God's guidance, perhaps in response to yes-or-no questions by the leaders of the people.

The word Urim means "lights." Thummim comes from a Hebrew word that signifies integrity. In the breastplate of the priest were light and integrity that guided the priests and Israel's rulers.

Ephesians 6:14 says to "put on the breastplate of righteousness." Righteousness works through integrity. In a sense, you can put on spiritual parallels of the Urim and Thummim. You can count on God's guidance as you live for Him in integrity and righteousness.

Psalm 84:11 says, "The Lord will give grace and glory; no good thing will He withhold from those who walk uprightly." The Lord can and does withhold His favor from those who choose sin's disintegrating influence. But when we walk in integrity we live a life that honors God. As a result we are honored by God and receive His favor. Honor God and He will honor you.

HUMILITY

God will bless the life of integrity. But the blessed believer must remain utterly dependent on the Lord. So often, after we have moved into a season of blessing and prosperity, we're tempted to take the credit for ourselves. God would remind us that He alone is the source of our righteousness, of all that is good in us.

Humility is absolutely essential to a life that honors God. "Before destruction the heart of a man is haughty, and before honor is humility" (Proverbs 18:12). Nobody ever desires destruction in their life, but because of their lack of character many people destroy their own lives. God will always promote and nurture humility in those who follow Him. And when believers allow that humility to grow, they encounter new levels of blessing. But it is not a simple process.

We are told, "Moses was very humble, more than all men who were on the face of the earth" (Numbers 12:3). But was this his natural inclination? I believe Moses' humility was the result of God's dramatic shaping of his life.

Moses was trained to the highest standards of education in ancient Egypt. He was a prince. Growing up in Egypt's palace, Moses would have been trained to become articulate, strong, and brave in battle. Moses appeared to have everything going for him. But if he had remained in Egypt's palace, he never would have amounted to anything of eternal significance.

When God was finished with Moses after 40 years in the desert, Moses was a different man. When God appeared to Moses in the burning bush and informed him of His plan to use him as Israel's deliverer, Moses replied, "Who am I that I should go to Pharaoh, and that I should bring the children of Israel out of Egypt?" (Exodus 3:11). And again, in the next chapter, Moses said, "O my Lord, I am not eloquent, neither before nor since you have spoken to your servant; but I am slow of speech and slow of tongue" (Exodus 4:10). Something in Moses had been broken. He had changed.

Are there circumstances in life you are trying to get out of? Things you don't want to even acknowledge? God may be developing humility in you in order to prepare you to serve Him in honor and favor. The apostle Paul prayed three times for God to remove the thorn in his flesh. God told Paul He was not going to remove it. Paul learned that when he was weak then he was truly strong (2 Corinthians 12:10).

Have you ever had a thorn in your life? Have you complained about it? Cursed it? Rebuked the devil over it? Prayed about it? The thorns in your life can keep you weak in yourself. That's OK. God's influence in your life is then at its strongest.

You may think as a believing, Bible-reading, faith-filled, praying person that you can remove any obstacle. Then you find an obstacle you can't get rid of. God will use any means necessary to remove the strength of the carnal nature so His power and grace can become the Christian's true strength . . . and ensure that God will get the glory. We learn that our weakness is a foundation for God's power.

In our early years of ministry, my wife, Jodi, and I believed that we were going to be elevated to greater places and positions of ministry. Things were going well. Instead, through a painful experience and unfair circumstances, we found ourselves in a place of obscurity. We complained to God and reminded Him of the vision He had placed in our hearts. It took some time for us to realize that God had not forgotten us. He was indeed at work, developing in us what would be needed for our future ministry. We learned that His grace is sufficient!

We found joy in serving God and not worrying about location, influence, or our desires. After several years God moved us into areas of greater influence and responsibility. Now in the midst of those opportunities I am uncomfortable, in many ways, because I recognize my weakness and dependency upon God. I am thankful that it keeps me walking close to Him.

God told Jeremiah to go to the potter's house and watch the

potter with the vessel. He was shaping it and there appeared a flaw. The potter broke the pot, crushed it and remade it. (See Jeremiah 18:1-6.) God may have to break something in order to have His way with a vessel. But even during those times of brokenness, the believer can find comfort. "The Lord is near to those who have a broken heart" (Psalm 34:18).

Remember the alabaster box filled with perfume mentioned in Mark 14:3? When broken, the perfume spilled everywhere and filled the whole room with a sweet smell. Everyone was amazed as the woman poured it on Jesus' head. After a life is broken, the sweet sense of Christ can flow over a person. Have you ever met someone with a sweet spirit? They may have come through horrible deserts that have crushed them.

The burning bush was a second chance for Moses. He learned that failure is a school that brings you into humility. The thorn in Paul's flesh taught him that God was strongest at his weakest point. Each of these "giants of the faith" felt small and weak and insignificant. Yet, look at how God used them.

As you walk closer to Jesus, in humility and with integrity, you will live a life that honors God. As a result He will bring honor to you.

R. Leigh Metcalf is an ordained minister with the Assemblies of God. He is the lead pastor at Bradshaw Mountain Christian Assembly in Prescott Valley, Arizona, a church he planted in 1997. He also serves as the Arizona District HonorBound Men's Director. Leigh attended Southwestern Assemblies of God University in Waxahachie, Texas, and Vanguard University in Costa Mesa, California. He has been married for 16 years to Jodi. They have two children: Caden, 13, and Brinlee, 11. Web site: www.bradshawmountain.org.

Section 2

"Faith is the activator and the channel for the miracles of Jesus; hope is the motivator that brings us to Jesus in the first place."

—Alton Garrison

Hope	Alton Garrison
Adversity	Glen Berteau
Pain	Lisa Clay
Emotions	Tim Olson
Peace	Mark Robinson

CHAPTER 6

Hold on to Hope

ALTON GARRISON

Jesus stood by the hot, dusty road, the sea behind Him. Throngs pushed and shoved, reaching and grasping to touch the Master. They had come with their children, with the elderly, with those on crutches. Some crawled to reach Him. Some came because of their need; others came to observe, particularly the religious scribes.

Jesus had just come from the country of the Gadarenes. He had just cast a legion of demons out of a madman there. Jesus' heart must have melted as He looked upon the people crying out in need . . . sheep without a shepherd. The disciples formed a tight circle around Jesus and escorted Him through the mass of bodies as the crowd shouted His name. "Jesus! Jesus, help me . . . have mercy on me . . . Jesus!"

Jairus, a man of prestige, was able to chisel his way through the wall of bodies. As he stood before the Master, he fell at Jesus' feet and pleaded, "My little daughter is dying. Please come and put your hands on her so that she will be healed and live" (Mark 5:23, NIV). Jesus consented; the people followed.

Hundreds of heartrending conditions were represented by that crowd, but only two were mentioned: Jairus' daughter and a woman who suffered with a chronic bleeding condition. For 12 long years she had gone to physician after physician—to no avail. She spent all she had and had only grown worse. Nothing remained except the determination only hope could produce. She had heard about the great miracles Jesus performed and believed He could heal her . . . if only He would.

Suddenly, the press of people thickened. Jesus was coming closer. *There He is! I can see Him! He's walking my way.*

Hope began to rise in her heart. If she could just touch Him, she would be healed. She knew it. Somehow, she pressed through that suffocating mass. With all her strength she reached for Him . . . until she touched the hem of His garment. *What is happening? Life is coming into my body. Strength is flowing through me. I feel strong. There is no pain! The bleeding . . .* She gasped. *There is no blood! The bleeding has stopped! I am whole! I am whole!*

"Who touched Me?" Jesus asked, turning to survey the crowd.

The disciples looked at Him in disbelief. They were nearly crushed by the crowd, and He wanted to know who touched Him?

"It was I," the woman said, quivering. "It was I." She fell at His feet, trembling, as the power of God continued to work in her body. Fear vanished as she looked into His eyes and told Him she had been healed when she touched His garment.

Meanwhile, Jairus shifted from one leg to another. Why didn't Jesus come with him? His daughter was near death; she could be dying this very moment. Didn't Jesus know how urgent it was? Why did He take so long with this woman?

The words of Jesus interrupted his thoughts. "Daughter, your faith . . . your trust and confidence in Me . . . has restored you to health. Go in . . . peace and be continually healed and free from your . . . disease" (Mark 5:34, Amplified).

While Jesus spoke, a group of men found Jairus. "Your daughter has died; come with us now. Why bother and distress the Teacher any further?"

Before Jairus could say a word, Jesus turned to him. "Do not be seized with alarm and have no fear, only keep on believing" (Mark 5:36).

HOPE DELAYED

Have you ever been in a desperate situation? Have you felt there was no cure, no help, no hope? Have you wrestled with despondency to such a degree that you wondered if God was still there?

In the small town of Bethany, right outside Jerusalem, lived a family Jesus dearly loved. Mary, Martha, and Lazarus had traveled extensively with Him. I can imagine the sisters had often gone before the Master, making the next town ready for His arrival. They had seen Him perform many miracles and were present when the multitude was fed and when He turned the water into wine. Often, they sat late into the night, listening to the profound teachings of Christ, the Son of God, their dearest friend.

And then tragedy struck. Lazarus was deathly ill.

"Martha, send word to the Master," Mary said. "I know He will come right away, and when He does our brother will recover and be healed." She had seen Jesus heal persons He had never met. Surely, as dearly as He loved Lazarus, He would stop everything and come to Lazarus' bedside.

She glanced toward her brother, who was already unconscious. *Everything will be fine soon.*

Martha, wanting to remain at Lazarus' side with Mary, sent trustworthy friends to Jerusalem to find Jesus. They left before dawn for the two-mile journey. Dawn turned into morning; morning eased into afternoon, but there was no sign of the Master. Mary paced before the window of Lazarus' room.

The afternoon passed with no word from Jesus. Suddenly, a knock at the door startled the sisters. They jumped up, expecting to welcome the Lord. Their hearts sank at what they saw. Their friends had returned . . . but where was Jesus?

"We told the Master," they said. "Jesus said to us, 'This sickness is not to end in death . . . but to glorify God.' "

Mary spoke first. "But where is He?"

The friends exchanged a glance. "He remained in Jerusalem. He didn't come back with us."

Three days later, at the entrance of their brother's tomb, Mary and Martha stood in a whirlwind of emotions. Doubt, anger, and fear fought to control them. *Why didn't Jesus come? Why did He let us down when we needed Him the most?*

Faith is imperative in such times of need. But what about hope? Without it, faith cannot produce the desired results. If we are to stand victorious in adverse situations, faith and hope must operate together.

Faith deals with details; hope deals with Deity. Faith finds its foundation in the Word; hope is a mental attitude. Faith is the activator and the channel for the miracles of Jesus; hope is the motivator that brings us to Jesus in the first place.

The story of the woman with the issue of blood, as told in Mark 5, is a classic example. She had faith, but hope put her on the road to health. "For whatsoever things were written aforetime were written for our learning, that we through patience and comfort of the scriptures might have hope" (Romans 15:4, KJV). In other words, the Word produces hope, which causes faith to rise, which brings results.

Hope is defined as "the feeling that what is wanted can be had or that events will turn out well." Faith is the dynamite that explodes truth and brings us from doubt into belief. Hope is the fuse that sets it off. Without a fuse, dynamite is worthless.

HOPE EMBRACED

The town of Shunem had been good for them. The Shunammite woman's husband was influential in the city, and they had prospered. They were hard workers who served people and respected God. The prophet Elisha passed through their city.

I hear this is a true man of God, the Shunammite woman thought. *If it is true, I want to serve him while he's in my city.*

She found Elisha and offered him a generous meal at her home. Elisha enjoyed the company of the woman and her husband, and he made it a practice to visit each time he was in their city. (See 2 Kings 4:8-17.)

Once, as Elisha rested in the room they had prepared for him, the Spirit of God prodded his heart. God wanted to bless the woman and her aged husband, who had no children.

"At this season next year," he told her, "you shall hold a son from your husband."

As Elisha had prophesied, she conceived and brought forth a child.

One day, there was a commotion. Her servants ran toward her—carrying her son! "The boy is sick!"

She held him close to her. As he cried in pain, she felt the shallowness of his breathing. Suddenly, the breathing stopped. Without a word, she carried him up the stairs, past her bedroom, past his room, and into the room they had built for Elisha. She laid him on the bed, shut the door, and turned to her servants. "Get me a donkey. I will go quickly to the man of God and come back again."

From a distance, Elisha could see the dust. "Look, Gehazi, there is the Shunammite woman. Run to meet her and ask if all is well."

Gehazi hurried to meet her as she slid off the donkey. "Is all well with your husband and son?" Gehazi asked.

"All is well," she replied, walking past him toward Elisha.

HOPE REWARDED

Why had she responded so? The hope inside her refused to give up. She knew God, and hope sent her straight to His prophet for a miracle.

Satan's attack may not be against our faith so much as our hope, for he knows hope is what takes us to faith. It is easier for him to discourage us emotionally than spiritually. But he cannot alter the Word of God. If we cling to His promises we need not be defeated by our circumstances.

The Shunammite woman refused to lose hope. After she told Elisha about the death of her son, Elisha sent Gehazi to raise him from the dead. It didn't work. She did not give up.

Then Elisha came and shut himself up with the woman's son. He did not come out of the room until the boy was restored to life. Hope in God's Word had produced the desired miracle.

TIME OF TESTING

Many persons around the world have believed God for a particular need, then, when the answer didn't come right away, they gave up. They lost hope. God not only wants to inspire our faith, He wants to rekindle our hope. Faith says, "He is able." Hope says, "He is willing."

God is willing to meet our needs. Often, there is a time lapse between the giving and fulfillment of God's promise. Imagine how Jairus felt. He made his way through the crowd, got Jesus' attention, and found Him willing to help. But they were pressed for time. Jairus' daughter was near death. The woman with the issue of blood had a need, but his daughter was dying! Then the news came; it was too late. Jesus had taken too much time with the woman.

Jairus was between the promise and the fulfillment of the promise. He was in the time of testing.

Fear robs our hope. It is a thief that paralyzes our faith. That is why Jesus addressed the fear issue first. "Fear not," He said, then added, "only believe." Jairus chose to do just that. He took the Son of God into his daughter's room and watched life come into her again.

What about Mary and Martha? Of course, they were disappointed that Jesus didn't come when they thought He should. After all, their brother's life was on the line. As Martha met Jesus, she grabbed His hand. She looked into His eyes, and all doubt disappeared. She did not understand it, but she spoke the truth when she said, "Master, if You had been here, my brother would not have died." In spite of the negative thoughts that assailed her, she remained faithful to the One she had served.

She ran back inside the house to tell Mary. Mary ran quickly, followed by the Jewish leaders.

Jesus walked up to the opening of the cold, dark tomb. "Take away the stone," He commanded. "Lazarus, come forth!" Immediately, Lazarus arose and walked into the daylight, still bound head and foot in grave clothes. Mary and Martha received their miracle, and many observers became believers.

It doesn't matter what the doctor says. It doesn't matter what the checkbook says. It doesn't matter how dismal the situation appears. God is willing to bring a miracle when it is needed. When He gives a promise, He will fulfill it.

DESTROYERS OF HOPE

There are three things that destroy hope. The first is *when we believe only what we see.* When the devil succeeds in making the circumstance seem bigger than the Creator, hope is lost. He brings fear, paralyzing our ability to believe. He lies to us; and his subtle ways make us vulnerable—if we take our eyes off Jesus. We must remember Jesus *promised* trouble would come our way. But He also promised never to leave us or forsake us.

Hope is also destroyed *when we battle God's promise.* What did Abraham think when God promised him a son—when God said his offspring would be as the sands of the sea? Abraham was 75 years old, and his wife 65. When Sarah first heard, she laughed. But Abraham knew God had the ability to do what He had promised, no matter how impossible it seemed. And, just as God had said, Sarah conceived a son.

Abraham did not have the written Word to offer strength, faith, and hope. He did not have fellowship with other believers. All he had was the promise of God. Every day he had to battle the lies of the enemy.

Unlike Abraham, we have both the written Word of God and the fellowship of the saints. We also have the same enemy that tempted Abraham to doubt. He still tries to convince us God's promises are not true. But we must remember, circumstances are not greater than the power of our God.

Third, hope is destroyed *when we become our own answer.* Waiting is the hardest thing to do. We devise ways to bring about what God said *He* would do, and we get ahead of Him.

Impatience leads to erratic behavior. We try one thing and it doesn't work; we do another and it doesn't work. The further we venture out on our own, the deeper the trouble becomes.

Abraham and Sarah fell into the trap of impatience and decided to "help God" fulfill His promise. Under Sarah's instruction, Abraham went to her servant and a son was conceived. When Sarah finally conceived the son of promise, she became jealous and demanded the woman and her son be sent away. God reprimanded Abraham for not waiting on God, but promised to care for the child. Abraham sent Ishmael and his mother away, but he missed his son and grieved over him. That grief remained with him the rest of his life. Like Abraham, when we attempt to solve problems in our own strength, we create "Ishmaels."

SOURCE OF HOPE

God has set the time for performing what He has promised. We have to wait for His time. Reading and believing the Word of God will produce hope and help us hold on while we wait on God, for God is the source of hope. "Now the *God* of hope fill you with all joy and peace in believing, that ye may abound in hope, through the power of the Holy Ghost" (Romans 15:13, KJV). Hope is only as good as its source. If God is the God of hope, we have nothing to worry about. God is in control. It doesn't matter what man says—only what God says.

No adversity can triumph over a hope-filled believer. There is no circumstance too great, no tragedy too heartbreaking, no affliction too devastating to conquer hope. Romans 8:31 says, "If God be for us, who can be against us?" What greater way can hope be quickened in us, than to know the Source of all good things is on our side?

Alton Garrison serves as executive director of Assemblies of God U.S. Missions. After serving as a member on the U.S. Missions board, he is keenly aware of challenges faced by the missionaries and chaplains. An executive presbyter for the last four years, Garrison served as superintendent of the Arkansas District from 2001 to 2005. He was pastor of First Assembly of God in North Little Rock, Arkansas, for 15 years. From 1966 to 1985, Garrison ministered as an evangelist. He now serves on multiple boards of directors.

Garrison's ministry emphasizes three distinct and important areas: evangelism, equipping, and encouraging. As a pastor in North Little Rock, he spearheaded extensive lay ministry involvement, which led the church in 1996 to give $1.4 million to missions.

Garrison and his wife, Johanna, have one daughter, Lizette. He authored the book Building a Winning Team *and was a contributing author to a prior Onward book,* Portraits of Success. *Mrs. Garrison has published* Tangled Destinies, *the story of God's faithfulness to her family.*

CHAPTER 7

The In-Between

GLEN BERTEAU

Read the opening chapters of Exodus and you encounter a summary of the suffering God's people endured in the land of Egypt. Since the days when Jacob and his sons arrived under the care of Joseph, the Children of Israel had multiplied to the point that a Pharaoh who lived generations after Joseph was troubled.

Pharaoh was convinced the Israelites' numbers had swelled so much that, if organized, they could overthrow him. So he subjected the Children of Israel to a severe captivity. They were brutalized and abused. Their children and grandchildren, born in Egypt, knew only slavery.

The people of God cried out to Him. God sent Moses, His deliverer. The rest of Exodus is a powerful narrative of God's mighty acts in behalf of His people against an oppressive world power. Ten plagues later, Egypt was on its knees and God's people were marching triumphantly toward Canaan.

PROMISED LAND, TESTING LAND

Some 40 years later, Moses commanded the Israelites to teach their children about that deliverance.

Deuteronomy 6:21 (NKJV): "Then you shall say to your son: 'We were slaves of Pharaoh in Egypt, and the Lord brought us out of Egypt with a mighty hand.' "

Christians could paraphrase that verse this way: "Many of us were slaves to the devil. We were bound and oppressed. We were born into this condition of spiritual bondage, but the Lord brought us out with a mighty hand."

Deuteronomy 6:23: "Then He brought us out from there, that He might bring us in, to give us the land of which He swore to our fathers."

At this point, the Israelites had not set foot in the land God had promised them. What they had done was face years of trial, years of coming to grips with what it means to serve God, years when the worst parts of their own nature were revealed and addressed.

We're in a similar situation. We have not yet arrived where God wants to bring us. We have been brought *out* if we have accepted Christ as our Savior, but we're really not *in* yet. This is the In-Between.

The promises of Scripture clearly reveal the first part of God's plan, our salvation, and the last part of His plan, our eternal future with Him. But God doesn't spell out everything that happens during the In-Between.

JOSEPH'S IN-BETWEEN

Think back to the circumstances that brought the Israelites into Egypt in the first place.

Jacob's son Joseph had two dreams (Genesis 37:5-9). One was about his brothers' bound stalks of wheat bowing down to his stalks during harvest. In the other dream, the sun, moon, and 11 stars bowed down before Joseph. Joseph was living in the first part of God's plan for his life, and God gave him a glimpse of the last part. But God didn't tell him the details of the In-Between.

God didn't tell Joseph about the "coat of many troubles." God didn't tell Joseph his brothers were going to despise him and drag him to a pit to die. God didn't tell Joseph he would be sold into slavery and placed in Potiphar's house, or that Potiphar's wife would proposition him and then lie about it. God said nothing to Joseph about the years in a dirty dungeon.

God told Joseph the first part. He gave Joseph hints through two powerful dreams that he was going to be a man of influence. But God didn't tell Joseph all the details—the In-Between. God doesn't tell us either.

OUR IN-BETWEEN

Just as God did not tell Joseph about his slavery or imprisonment, or the Israelites about their 40-year trek through the wilderness, neither has He told you the details of the In-Between where you will walk through untold situations.

God didn't tell you you're going to struggle to pay your bills. He didn't tell you you're going to walk through a divorce. He didn't tell you you're going to lose a child. He didn't alert you that you're going to lose your job. He didn't tell you you're going to walk through some kind of cancer. He didn't tell you the details of this trip called the In-Between. We've been brought *out* but we have yet to be brought *in*.

When I got saved, God brought me out. I was overjoyed to experience the first part. Salvation was great. Then, after just a couple of weeks, God gave me a concluding part to His vision for my life and ministry. God told me, *I'm going to help you win a city.* But He didn't tell me about the In-Between.

God didn't tell me that my wife, Debbie, and I would have to live in 14 houses along this trip. He didn't tell me I would have to sell my graduation and football rings to a pawn shop just to pay the bills when we started in the ministry. God didn't tell me that our three kids would be born in three different states. He didn't tell me that my sister would die of ovarian cancer. He didn't tell me that my oldest daughter, at age 16, would suffer with rheumatoid arthritis. God didn't tell me the In-Between. All He told me was, *I'm going to bring you out and you're going to win a city.* But I didn't get the details of the In-Between.

We struggle with the things God *doesn't* tell us. But all of us are going to walk through suffering. All of us are going to walk through some pain. That is part of life's journey. The wilderness was not a fun place to live and travel. But that was where the Children of Israel had to go to make it to the Promised Land.

OUR PROMISED LAND

We are all in the In-Between. God brought us out but we haven't arrived yet. We're not in heaven yet. What we do during the In-Between is what we're going to be judged for. God is going to judge our lives.

Anticipating His evaluation of our lives should affect our motivation and commitment. Just going to church is not enough. You can say, "I'm going to church" just as casually as "I'm going to the movies." If you're not doing something with what you're learning, then you're not changing. When we get to heaven, God will look carefully at our commitment to Him during our time of testing—right here in the In-Between.

1 Corinthians 3:13: "Each one's work will become clear; for the Day will declare it, because it will be revealed by fire; and the fire will test each one's work, of what sort it is."

God's holy fire will determine if our work holds any of the lasting value God intends our lives to have. God says, *I want to see if Glen Berteau's life had any value between the time that I took him out and the time that I brought him home. Is there anything valuable in his life?*

1 Corinthians 9:24,25: "Do you not know that those who run in a race all run, but one receives the prize? Run in such a way that you may obtain it. And everyone who competes for the prize is temperate in all things. Now they do it to obtain a perishable crown, but we for an imperishable crown."

The reward is a crown. You may ask, "Do you mean I'm running this whole race, with everything I'm going through in my life, and when I make it, I'm going to get a crown? That's *all* I get? What's the deal?" You're going to find out it's a *big* deal!

OUR TESTING, HIS CROWN

Revelation 3:11: "Behold, I am coming quickly! Hold fast what you have, that no one may take your crown."

Jesus is saying that someone can take your crown. Who wants to take it? The devil wants to take your crown, your reward. He doesn't want you to do anything in the In-Between that will make a difference for the Kingdom. Satan doesn't want you to discover your potential. He doesn't want you to have any value at all. He attacks your crown by getting you to complain and become taken up by the cares and issues of this life. The devil is fighting to take not only your life, but your reward, your crown, as well.

The first crown that Jesus wore was a crown of thorns. Before we get the crown of victory and triumph, there's going to be some pain connected to this In-Between time. But we conquer. As we do what God has commanded, as we serve Him with every part of our being, we move steadily toward the day we receive a crown.

Revelation 4:4: "Around the throne were twenty-four thrones, and on the thrones I saw twenty-four elders sitting, clothed in white robes; and they had crowns of gold on their heads."

God is not going to give every believer the same crown. This is not "one size fits all." There are crowns of victory and triumph. If you win souls, you will receive a crown of soul winning. Stephen the martyr was faithful to the end. There are people today being told to denounce Christ or die. They refuse and suffer the consequences. They will receive crowns of martyrdom and faithfulness. Many of you had to leave behind family and homeland to serve God. There is a crown of separation for you. Others, having endured great suffering and pain while remaining faithful to Christ, will receive a crown that honors that suffering.

Revelation 4:9,10: "Whenever the living creatures give glory and honor and thanks to Him who sits on the throne, who lives forever and ever, the twenty-four elders fall down before Him who sits on the throne and worship Him who lives forever and ever, and cast their crowns before the throne."

You and I, like the 24 elders, will cast our crowns before the throne. I will give my crown back to the One who gave me the power to receive it. I'll lay my crown at Christ's feet and say, "Lord, thank You for everything You've done in my life. Thank You for changing me and saving me. Thank You for never leaving me or forsaking me during my In-Between time."

I'll see the millions who have suffered, who have been martyred, who have been faithful and lived for God. They will also cast their crowns at His feet.

When Jesus comes back on a white horse, Revelation 19:12 says, "On His head [will be] many crowns." I believe Christ's crowns represent something powerful about your life and mine. Those crowns represent our endurance and the souls we have won to Christ between the time He brought us out until the time He brings us to heaven. Those crowns represent our victory and triumph and how we conquered in this place called the In-Between.

Glen Berteau is senior pastor of Calvary Temple Worship Center in Modesto, California, a church of 3,000.

Outreaches at Calvary Temple, including 12 years of present-ing the drama Heaven's Gates and Hell's Flames, *have resulted in more than 110,000 people won to the Lord.* Berteau's book When God Shakes a City *(Gospel Publishing House, 1997) documents a significant portion of that revival.*

Berteau is a veteran church planter. CTWC has established outreach churches to the Assyrian, Messianic, Cambodian, Hispanic and Russian communities in Modesto, as well as a church in Seattle, Washington, and three additional churches in California.

Berteau is president of Global Bible Institute, a ministerial training school that has majors in children, youth, music, missions, counseling and pastoral ministries. He is president/founder of 4:15 Apostolic International, a mentoring ministry to church leaders, and founder of D-12, a mentoring strategy based on groups of 12 pastors. Berteau's Send7enty ministry gathers 70 youth pastors from across the country for mentoring conferences. Glen Berteau Ministries is a nonprofit ministry at CTWC that distributes all of Berteau's personal ministry material (www. glenberteau.com).

Glen has ministered as a speaker, teacher, and evangelist at conferences, churches, camps, and conventions all over the world. In his youth ministry days he pastored one of the largest youth ministries in the nation, with 1,500 at Wednesday night youth services. Berteau published Strategies for Advancing Youth Ministry *in 1994.*

Berteau holds a master's degree in pastoral ministries and a graduate teacher certificate from Trinity Theological Seminary, Newburgh, Indiana.

Glen and Deborah Berteau have been married for 31 years. Deborah founded Deborah's Army, an intercessory prayer group at CTWC. She also mentors 30 women in their home. The Berteaus have three grown children: Kelli Williams, Christy Johnson and Micah Berteau. His daughters are married to pastors at Calvary Temple, where they also serve. Micah is attend-ing college and also serves at Calvary Temple.

CHAPTER 8

The Pain of Injustice and the Promise of Intervention

LISA CLAY

"But let justice roll on like a river, righteousness like a never-failing stream!" (Amos 5:24, NIV).

Injustice: After almost 20 years of marriage, Jason* abandoned his wife, Tricia*, and their three children to pursue a lifetime hobby of hunting and fishing. He didn't show up for his son's high school graduation, and he is doing next to nothing to support them financially. Tricia is a devoted follower of Jesus, yet her car is being repossessed and her home threatened with foreclosure.

Injustice: Adam*, a faithful, hardworking pastor, was accused by a church member and a disgruntled deacon of spending a large amount of money without permission. Their false accusations brought Adam an untold degree of heartache, wounding his good name and reputation. The two men never repented and never apologized.

Injustice: Sarah Johnson, a worker at our local boys/girls detention center, was suspended without pay because a young girl accused Sarah of sexually molesting her. Sarah was arrested, handcuffed and jailed, and then released on a $20,000 bond. She was without a job as Christmas approached, and she and her two children had to move to a cheaper apartment to afford rent. She waitressed to meet her bills, all the time maintaining her innocence. Seven months later, the young girl sent a letter to the police admitting that no sexual molestation had occurred.

Sarah, commenting to our local newspaper, said, "I felt bewildered and betrayed throughout the ordeal. I didn't understand why this was being done to me in the first place. I feel anger and sadness that she could do this to someone."

Sarah will get her job back once the criminal charges are dismissed, and she will also receive back pay for the time she was off work. At last report she was eager to seek reinstatement and get her family's life back to normal.[1]

YOU ARE IN GOOD COMPANY

There is no pain as sharp or as startling as the pain caused by injustice. One dictionary describes it as "suffering hardship or loss undeservingly." We flinch when we recall the injustices we've endured, wondering privately if we will ever experience vindication in the matter. Injustice is profoundly challenging, striking us when we least expect it, wounding our mind and emotions. We recoil at its bite, feeling violated and abused and powerless.

Most of us secretly hold fast to the idea that if we live a righteous life and do our best to serve God, we will be spared the agony of injustice. After all, we muse, why would God allow someone else's wrongdoing to wreak havoc in my life when I am doing everything I can to live for Him?

Yet injustice arrives anyway, often cloaked and unannounced, and carries out its venomous deed. Our hearts rage, and doubt sweeps us out into the sea of abandonment. "Unfair!" we shout at God. "I have done nothing to deserve this! You have forsaken me!" Our cries seem swallowed up by an endless ocean of unanswered questions.

As if on cue, a chorus of ancient voices echoes our desperate cries:

Jeremiah the prophet, the man of tears, cries out to God, "I would speak with you about your justice: Why does the way of the wicked prosper?" (Jeremiah 12:1).

Habakkuk, deeply distressed at the injustice sweeping his country, writes, "Justice never prevails. The wicked hem in the righteous, so that justice is perverted" (Habakkuk 1:4).

Job, our example of innocent suffering, cries out repeatedly that he is suffering injustice. "Though I cry, 'I've been wronged!' I get no response; though I call for help, there is no justice. . . . As surely as God lives, who has denied me justice . . . I am innocent, but God denies me justice" (Job 19:7; 27:2; 34:5).

The fiercely passionate Isaiah reveals the emotional toll exacted by injustice: "We all growl like bears; we moan mournfully like doves. We look for justice, but find none; for deliverance, but it is far away"(Isaiah 59:11).

YOU ARE ON GOD'S MIND

Our cries blend with these voices from long ago, wrestling and agonizing over the mystery of justice withheld. In the face of all our questions, God speaks through His Word, guaranteeing justice for you and for me, and for all who call Him Father. Isaiah writes reassuringly, "Yet the Lord longs to be gracious to you; he rises to show you compassion. For the Lord *is* a God of justice. Blessed are all who *wait* for him!" (Isaiah 30:18, emphasis mine).

"Wait" is a curse word to most of us. When we experience injustice, waiting to be vindicated seems like torture. The bad guy is running free while I suffer for his sins! Unbelievable! The unfairness of it all leaves us sleepless and fretful. We wonder why any time at all has to elapse between our offender's evil deed and divine retribution.

Yet there is divine wisdom hidden in the waiting. You can be sure God has *seen* all that has transpired in your life, and that every detail of your ordeal is laid bare before Him. "But you, O God, do see trouble and grief; you consider it to take it in hand. The victim commits himself to you" (Psalm 10:14). God has *heard* your many cries: "You hear, O Lord, the desire of the afflicted; you encourage them, and you listen to their cry" (Psalm 10:17). God *remembers* what has been done to you: "For he who avenges blood remembers; he does not ignore the cry of the afflicted" (Psalm 9:12).

God is not intentionally extending your pain by delaying His justice. In His wisdom He is watching and waiting, measuring the heart, thoughts, intentions, and actions of the one who has injured you, searching for genuine repentance, giving opportunity for the offender to initiate apology and restitution. He grants you and me the same privilege when we are the ones at fault. He calls it *mercy,* and He extends it even to the least deserving troublemaker. (Why is it we seem to want mercy for our own sins, and justice for the sins of others?)

Even though it isn't necessarily easy, it is possible for you to peacefully wait for divine justice, knowing that God has very purposefully restrained His hand of judgment in your case. He is not neglecting or forgetting justice. He is keenly aware of the amount of time that has elapsed since you were mistreated. And there will be a moment, one known only to God, when time will have run out, and God's justice will be meted out in full measure on your unrepentant offender. And that thought, instead of bringing joy, should bring you and me to our knees in humility before the Righteous Judge, knowing we ourselves are also deserving of His holy justice.

Make no mistake, in the midst of your pain and heartache, about the passion your Father has to see you receive justice. At least three times in Scripture our Father says He *loves* justice (Psalm 11:7; 33:5; Isaiah 61:8). The Hebrew word for love indicates a strong, deep, intimate affection, and the Hebrew word for justice means a verdict, pronounced as a sentence, including the act, the place, the suit, the crime and the penalty.[2] The Most Holy God, upright in all His ways, *loves* to carry out justice for you in minute detail, forgetting nothing, fairly imposing punishment upon the guilty and reward upon the innocent. When you are at your wits' end, with difficult memories pressing in upon you, remember that you only *desire* justice, but your Father *loves* justice. And He'll move heaven and earth to see that you get it. (See Psalm 18.)

YOU ARE ON A JOURNEY

My friend, have you ever considered that your struggle, instead of destroying you, may be a divine, predetermined doorway to a great personal triumph? Joseph, once incarcerated in Pharaoh's prison for resisting a sexual tryst with Potiphar's wife, must have regularly driven his exalted governor's chariot past Potiphar's house and the evil seductress herself. How she must have bowed low to Joseph, casting her eyes to the ground in fear and trembling!

During his season of suffering, Joseph's faith was anchored in God's promises to him, promises that God fulfilled to a degree unimaginable to Joseph during his darkest moments. Smith Wigglesworth, the great man of faith, once testified, "Great faith is the product of great fights. Great testimonies are the outcome of great tests. Great triumphs can only come out of great trials."[3] Joseph's lofty position required a lengthy, painful preparation. But when his suffering ended, Joseph was granted justice, reward, honor and victory in one explosive moment of promotion.

Remember, the injustice you have endured is trumped by God's unchangeable proclamation that "in all things God works for the good of those who love him, who have been called according to *his* purpose" (Romans 8:28). *His* ultimate purpose for your life may require you to undergo the salting season of injustice. If that is so, there is no way you can avoid your particular hour of suffering. Yet, be comforted knowing that when the time comes for justice to prevail and for you to be exalted in victory, it will happen seamlessly, accompanied by miracles and supernatural workings. Your testimony will mirror the apostle Paul's, who said, "What has happened to me will turn out for my deliverance," "what has happened to me has really served to advance the gospel" (Philippians 1:19,12).

A friend of mine—I'll call her Melissa—has walked through a very difficult and unjust circumstance. Her father, a well-known minister, author, and speaker, passed away. On the day of his funeral her father's ministry board asked the family to provide immediate copies of the ministry's financial statements. At the same time, a man her father had asked to resign from the board a year earlier was re-elected to the board.

Between the funeral and the reception, Melissa and her husband stood in a hotel office making photocopies of the financials. Melissa recalled her emotions, saying, "The emotional pain was enormous, and the injustice was severe, yet we did as asked in hope that we would be seen as being helpful and compliant."

Six weeks after the memorial service, the board fired almost every member of this ministry family and changed the locks on the ministry's building. Inside the building on the day they were fired were her father's lifetime collection of copies of his books, and also every picture her family had of their dad, which had been used to create a memorial video. Melissa still has not received these treasured photographs back, despite a signed settlement agreeing the items would be returned to the family.

I asked Melissa whether her extraordinarily difficult situation had a silver lining, a benefit that she had not expected. This was her response: "I believe that the sum total of our lives is never measured by what happens to us, but by what we do with what happens. Every opportunity that comes our way, whether positive or negative, when submitted to the Cross, becomes an occasion for victory. That's the nature of grace, and the transcendent glory of God that turns every difficulty into triumph. Every opportunity to die to our flesh is a good opportunity. That includes every trial, temptation, setback, embarrassment, and attack. If it causes us to sit back and become smaller, while Christ in us becomes bigger, it is the best thing that can happen to us. God is about the process, not just the product, of our lives."

No one suffered greater injustice than Jesus. He understands, and He will walk with you through your trial. Suffering friend, trust God and keep on trusting Him. He sees, hears, and remembers your story. Justice is on its way to you.

*Names have been changed.

Rev. Lisa Clay is the author of Rescued From Darkness, *a book for new believers with a foreword by the late Dr. Bill Bright (available on amazon.com). She and her husband, Rich, have senior pastored since 1988 at Bethany Assembly of God in Adrian, Michigan.*

The Clays are co-founders of Mountaintop Ministries (www.mountaintopministries.org) where Lisa serves as president. Lisa is on the Global Pastors' Wives Network Executive Board. She has two boys, Jared and Wesley. She is a speaker, a teacher, and is called to train, mentor, and encourage Christian leaders from every walk of life.

CHAPTER 9

Managing Our Emotions: Five Foundational Facts

TIM OLSON

One look at Jason and Loree* made it clear what was about to unfold in our upcoming counseling session. Loree entered my office with a look of frantic desperation—bloodshot, teary eyes, smudged mascara, furrowed brow, disheveled hair. Her husband, Jason, on the other hand, looked like what I imagined his driver's license photo probably looked like—stoic, no emotion, utterly disinterested. The scene was all too familiar.

My suspicions were quickly confirmed. I spent the next hour listening to Loree unload a truckload of assumptions, accusations, and exaggerations while Jason stared blankly at the wall behind me. I could tell by the look on his face that he had heard this well-rehearsed tirade before. When I did manage to sneak in an occasional question for Jason, he begrudgingly offered up responses of three words or fewer. The whole experience was sheer torture—one person with emotions that were out of control and the other who had shut down his emotions completely.

These two emotional extremes are quite common. I am constantly running into people whose unhealthy management of their emotions dominates their lives . . . some because their emotions run unchecked and some because their emotions have checked out. When it comes to emotions, many Christians find themselves unbalanced. Some Christians have a tendency to be very emotion driven, while others live in denial of their emotions and call it "spiritual maturity."

The following biblical facts can help us form a scriptural foundation for dealing with emotions in a healthy way.

EMOTIONS ARE A GIFT FROM GOD

People often live in denial of their emotions because they lack scriptural understanding. Christian men easily give in to our society's "macho man" image that has nothing to do with biblical masculinity. Some Christians adopt a view that emotions are evil and therefore should be extinguished and replaced with sound logic. All of us have been influenced by the level of emotions that were displayed or allowed in the homes we were raised in. The practice of denying our emotions, however, is not only unhealthy, it's unscriptural.

"So God created man in his own image, in the image of God he created him; male and female he created them" (Genesis 1:27, NIV). We are created in the image of God in order to bear His image for His glory. In fact, after God looked at His divine handiwork, He declared it was "very good" (Genesis 1:31). As creatures whose purpose is to bear God's own glorious image, we are created with emotions because God has emotions.

- God loves. (1 John 4:8; Romans 5:8; John 15:12)
- God has compassion. (Matthew 9:36,37; Mark 1:41; Luke 7:13; Exodus 33:19; Deuteronomy 13:17)
- God grieves. (Mark 3:5; Genesis 6:6)
- God gets angry. (Deuteronomy 3:26; 9:8; Psalm 7:11)

- God rejoices. (Isaiah 62:5; Luke 10:21)
- God weeps. (John 11:33,35)
- God laughs. (Psalm 2:4; 37:13; 59:8)

I am a little hesitant to say that God is emotional, because the word *emotional*, in many of our minds, connotes somebody who is not in control of himself. But the fact remains that God created us with emotions like His own and then said that this was "very good." A real key in getting a healthy grip on our emotions is to recognize that emotions are not evil; they are actually "very good." And, while uncontrolled emotions may lead to destructive thoughts and behaviors, denying our emotions is to deny the wisdom and goodness of God's plan at creation. When we shut down our emotions, we actually cease to display the wonder of God's glorious image.

OUR EMOTIONS ARE DAMAGED BY SIN

When sin entered the human experience, negative emotions entered the human soul for the first time. Genesis 3:7-10 says:

"Then the eyes of both of them were opened, and they realized they were naked; so they sewed fig leaves together and made coverings for themselves. Then the man and his wife heard the sound of the Lord God as he was walking in the garden in the cool of the day, and they hid from the Lord God among the trees of the garden. But the Lord God called to the man, 'Where are you?' He answered, 'I heard you in the garden, and I was afraid because I was naked; so I hid.' "

Because Adam and Eve were never intended for sin or the curse of sin, they began to deal with the destructive power of unhealthy emotions. Within moments of their disobedience, they were already beginning to display shame and fear. The next several chapters of Genesis, we find the following negative emotions that manifested after sin entered God's creation:

- Discord
- Jealousy
- Anger
- Rage
- Depression
- Anxiety
- Loneliness

As people began to give in to their negative impulses, emotions gained a stronger influence in the human soul. People were no longer in control of themselves. Rather, they were being controlled by their emotional impulses. This has had devastating results throughout history. The first murder took place in only the second generation of human existence, when Cain killed his brother Abel. The elevated influence of emotions on the human soul has brought destruction ever since.

Our emotions remain healthy when they are in balance with our mind and our will. When emotions become predominant over our mind and our will, we get into trouble. The word *emotion* comes from the Latin *emotio*, meaning "to move from." When our emotions become the "movers and shakers" of our lives, bad things happen. "Whoever has no rule over his own spirit is like a city broken down, without walls" (Proverbs 25:28, NKJV).

CHRIST UNDERSTANDS OUR EMOTIONS

We serve a God who understands us more than we even understand ourselves. Whether you're a person who tends to let your emotions ride on your sleeve, or you're a person who has walled yourself in beyond human reach, God understands and cares. He sees how the pain and cruelty of this world wreak havoc upon your soul. He hears the sharp words that pierce your heart. He knows about the abuse, the mistreatment, and the simple carelessness of others that have caused you to withdraw into your own emotional prison. He sees it all, knows it all, understands it all. And He cares more than you will ever know.

"For as high as the heavens are above the earth, so great is his love for those who fear him; as far as the east is from the west, so far has he removed our transgressions from us. As a father has compassion on his children, so the Lord has compassion on those who fear him; for he knows how we are formed, he remembers that we are dust" (Psalm 103:11-14, NIV).

CHRIST HAS THE POWER TO HEAL OUR EMOTIONS

God is in the restoration business. His promise to make us "new creations" (2 Corinthians 5:17) applies to the entirety of our being—body, soul, and spirit. It is God's very nature to heal. It's who He is. He has revealed himself as Yahweh Rapha, "The Lord Who Heals." In Exodus 15:22-25, God revealed His nature to Moses and the Israelites:

"Then Moses led Israel from the Red Sea and they went into the Desert of Shur. For three days they traveled in the desert without finding water. When they came to Marah, they could not drink its water because it was bitter. (That is why the place is called Marah.) So the people grumbled against Moses, saying, 'What are we to drink?'

"Then Moses cried out to the Lord, and the Lord showed him a piece of wood. He threw it into the water, and the water became sweet."

What an awesome promise for us today! The "bitter waters" that we have drunk in our past can be made "sweet" again through the wooden cross of Jesus. "He heals the brokenhearted and binds up their wounds" (Psalm 147:3). "A bruised reed he will not break, and a smoldering wick he will not snuff out" (Isaiah 42:3).

Jesus was broken for us. He was bruised for us. In Christ, God takes us bruised and broken and makes us whole again.

The following is a declaration of faith that I call The

Champion's Creed. I have our entire congregation read it aloud together from time to time. Every time we do this, strongholds are broken as the power of God's truth is applied to our lives.

The Champion's Creed

Yes . . . I can believe.
"I tell you the truth, if you have faith as small as a mustard seed, you can say to this mountain, 'Move from here to there' and it will move. Nothing will be impossible for you" (Matthew 17:20).

Yes . . . I can change.
"And we, who with unveiled faces all reflect the Lord's glory, are being transformed into his likeness with ever-increasing glory, which comes from the Lord, who is the Spirit" (2 Corinthians 3:18).

Yes . . . I can love and be loved.
"By this all men will know that you are my disciples, if you love one another" (John 13:35).

Yes . . . I can forgive and be forgiven.
"Be kind and compassionate to one another, forgiving each other, just as in Christ God forgave you" (Ephesians 4:32).

Yes . . . I can rule my thought life.
"And the peace of God, which transcends all understanding, will guard your hearts and your minds in Christ Jesus. Finally, brothers, whatever is true, whatever is noble, whatever is right, whatever is pure, whatever is lovely, whatever is admirable—if anything is excellent or praiseworthy—think about such things" (Philippians 4:7,8).

Yes . . . I can control my emotions.
"For God did not give us a spirit of timidity, but a spirit of power, of love and of self-discipline" (2 Timothy 1:7).

Yes . . . I can accomplish great things.
"I can do everything through him who gives me strength"
(Philippians 4:13).

Yes . . . I can resist temptation.
"No temptation has seized you except what is common
to man. And God is faithful; he will not let you be tempted
beyond what you can bear. But when you are tempted, he will
also provide a way out so that you can stand up under it"
(1 Corinthians 10:13).

Yes . . . I can overcome Satan.
"Submit yourselves, then, to God. Resist the devil, and he
will flee from you" (James 4:7).

THE SPIRIT GIVES US POWER TO STAY IN CONTROL

The secret of healthy emotions is not to deny or suppress our
emotions; the key is to allow our emotions to flourish under
the guidance of God's Spirit. "The fruit of the Spirit is . . . self
control" (Galatians 5:22,23). Paul encouraged Timothy by
reminding him, "God did not give us a spirit of timidity, but a
spirit of power, of love and of self-discipline" (2 Timothy 1:7).
If you want to control your emotions more, surrender more.
Allow God's Spirit to reign in your emotions. Feed on His
Word. Fellowship with His people. Grow in His grace. And live
in emotional victory!

*Names have been changed.

*Tim Olson has been an Assemblies of God minister since
1983. He has been the lead pastor of Bethel Church in
Medford, Oregon, since 1998. Tim and his wife, Janice, have
been married for 24 years and are the parents of three children:
Stephen (5/9/86), Stephanie (6/23/88), and Jennifer (7/20/91).*

Tim has earned a B.A. in pastoral ministries from Northwest University and an M.A. in biblical studies and theology from Fuller Theological Seminary.

CHAPTER 10

Peace in the Midst of the Storm

MARK ROBINSON

The surge of severe weather-related catastrophes that have hit the United States and around the world in recent years has people searching for the perfect place to live. One study, which was partially scientific and partially opinion, determined that the safest place to live in the United States is Blanding, a small town in southern Utah.[1]

Yet, even in Blanding—where most days you don't have to worry about floods, hurricanes, tornados, extreme winds, tsunamis, blizzards, earthquakes, or forest fires—there are "storms" that suddenly blow into residents' lives. Everyone is hit by some kind of storm. It might be the unexpected death of someone you love, or a major accident or injury. You may encounter struggles in your relationships or have problems at work or school. The doctor may detect a serious sickness or even diagnose a terminal illness. You may experience a devastating financial setback or suffer a crisis of your faith in God.

It would be amazing if we could find a place of perfect peace. But peace is not a place. Rather, it's a state of the heart built on your relationship with Christ. As such, it's possible to experience a profound sense of peace even while a storm rages all around you.

BIG STORM, BIGGER GOD

One day Jesus was with His disciples on the sea in a storm (Luke 8:22-25). Even though Jesus was with them in their fishing boat, they were overcome with fear. While the vicious storm pounded their craft, Jesus slept peacefully. The boat began to take on water and was in severe danger of becoming swamped. And Jesus . . . well, He was enjoying a power nap. The disciples became so fearful that they woke Jesus up with the news they were about to drown. Jesus rubbed the sleepiness from His eyes, rebuked the wind and the waves, and the storm immediately subsided.

Then Jesus calmly turned to the disciples and asked them a pointed question—"Where is your faith?" The disciples had faith; the problem was, it was focused on the storm. They had faith they were about to die!

What do you say when you are inside a storm? Where is your faith focused? I have a suggestion. Instead of telling God how big your storm is, why not tell your storm how big your God is!

When you are in the middle of a storm and realize your weakness to control the elements, it's prime time for Jesus Christ to display His power. Peter, the fisherman who became a disciple, wrote: "Dear friends, do not be surprised at the painful trial you are suffering, as though something strange were happening to you. But rejoice that you participate in the sufferings of Christ, so that you may be overjoyed when his glory is revealed" (1 Peter 4:12,13, NIV).

Did you catch what Peter said? Our weakness is an opportunity for Christ's greatness!

TRUTH, NOT TRUISMS

When people around you become aware that you are engaged in a personal storm they will often attempt to offer words of encouragement and comfort. Their intentions are good. They may counsel you to simply "hang in there" or offer the amplified version: "If you're at the end of your rope, tie a knot and hold on."

I don't know about you, but personally, I don't find these types of suggestions very helpful. If the storm has been sustained for any length of time, I have been holding on and I am getting tired. Extremely tired! I am starting to question whether I can survive. My mind is muddled with thoughts of despair and defeat that threaten to dominate my day and disrupt my sleep.

The perseverance necessary to survive storms is not a matter of playing brain games. It is not an exercise of self-help talk where you attempt to convince yourself you will live to see another day. It is not telling yourself over and over and over again that you are in a place of peace, even while you are languishing and growing weaker by the moment.

Though peace is not a place, peace *is* a Person. If you and I are going to successfully survive the storms of life, we have to seek this Person, the Prince of Peace, Jesus Christ (John 14:27).

NOW, NOT LATER

Too often people turn to Christ only because there is trouble in their lives. They don't sincerely want to follow Christ; they simply want to get out of the storm. If Jesus would just toss them a life preserver and bring them to a place of safety, they could go on with living their lives.

It's extremely important to learn what it means to walk in a relationship with Christ—you don't pursue that relationship because you need Christ to rescue you from a storm, but because you love Him. He wants to be your Peace, and so much more! As you learn how to pursue Christ in the middle of a storm you will discover the strength to persevere.

Paul made a profound statement in Romans 8:38,39: "For I am convinced that neither death nor life, neither angels nor demons, neither the present nor the future, nor any powers, neither height nor depth, nor anything else in all creation, will be able to separate us from the love of God that is in Christ Jesus our Lord."

Paul didn't need peace on the outside in order to have peace on the inside. Why? Because he was convinced that there was no storm so great that it could separate him from the love of Christ Jesus.

LITTLE STORMS, BIG TROUBLE

There is an additional reason why storms are so severe for some people. Before the "big one" arrives on the scene, there is a storm before the storm. Let me explain. Many people live with an inner storm within their soul. This turmoil leads to a constant condition of unsettledness and restlessness. The cause of this inner storm can be directly connected to a lack of peace in Christ. We must crave that relationship and its peace. Just look at how many times Paul prayed his readers would experience God's peace (Romans 15:13,33; 1 Corinthians 1:3; 2 Corinthians 1:2; Galatians 1:3 and others).

An inner storm may be the result of unforgiveness, unresolved hurt, questions about God's involvement or lack of involvement in your life, or the lack of an eternal perspective. This inner turmoil often produces waves of discontent, dissatisfaction, and discouragement, and can lead to anger, fear, anxiety, stress, and other very destructive emotions. If you lack peace before the storm hits, there's no way you are going to have peace during the storm.

The answer to surviving the storms that will inevitably blow into your life lies in developing your relationship with the Person who is the Prince of Peace. The best time to prepare for storms is before they arrive on the scene.

In John Ortberg's book *If You Want to Walk on Water, You've Got to Get Out of the Boat,* he cites a medical study that evaluated 122 men who had suffered their first heart attack. They were evaluated on their degree of hopefulness and pessimism. Here's what the study revealed:

- Of the 25 most pessimistic men, 21 had died eight years later.
- On the other hand, of the 25 most optimistic, only 6 had died!

Loss of hope increased the odds of death by 60 percent; it predicted death more accurately than any other medical risk factor, including blood pressure, amount of damage to the heart, or cholesterol level.

ALWAYS WITH YOU, ALWAYS FAITHFUL

Whatever happens in your life's circumstances, always remember that storms don't have the final say in your life. Repeat these words: "Storms don't have the final say in my life!"

When Jesus calmed the storm (Luke 8; Mark 4) the very next thing that happened was a supernatural demonstration of God's power—a demon-possessed man was set free. Jesus calmed the storm that was raging on the Sea of Galilee and then He turned and calmed the spiritual storm that was raging in the man from the region of the Gerasenes. The Prince of Peace stands prepared to speak to the storm in your life today. He promises to stay close enough to you to hear every whispered prayer and every whimper of fear.

Dr. Tony Campolo tells a story from his childhood growing up in a large city. His mother was concerned for his safety, so she asked a teenage neighbor girl to walk home with him from school each day. Tony's mom paid her a nickel a day to be his personal bodyguard. When Tony reached the second grade, he rebelled, because he believed he was big enough he didn't need anyone to walk with him. So, he told his mom to pay him a nickel a week, and he would be very careful each day walking home from school, and she could keep the extra 20 cents. After pleading and begging, Tony finally got his way. For the next two years he walked himself back and forth to school each day. It was an eight-block walk with many streets to cross, but Tony was always careful to look both ways, never talk to strangers, or get distracted.

Years later at a family party, Tony was bragging about how he used to walk home from school each day by himself. His mother laughed. "Did you really think you were alone?" she asked. "Every morning when you left for school, I left with you. I walked behind you all the way. When you got out of school at 3:30 in the afternoon, I was there. I always kept myself hidden, but I was there and I followed you all the way home. I just wanted to be there in case you needed me."

Regardless of the storm that you may be facing in your life, the Prince of Peace is never far away. He possesses the authority to control and calm the wind and the waves. With Jesus in your boat you are going to survive the storm.

Mark B. Robinson is the lead pastor of King Mountain Church (kingmountain.org) in Bellingham, Washington. Mark has been in full-time pastoral ministry since 1982, serving churches in Washington, Oregon, and Michigan. He graduated from Northwest University (Kirkland, Washington) in 1982. Mark's life mission is to "serve God's purposes with passion." He and his wife, Anita, have three daughters: Rochelle, Briana, and Kristen.

Section 3

"Where is your security? True wisdom declares it to be in a living relationship with God."
—Glen D. Cole

Wisdom	Glen D. Cole
Help	Terry Inman
Change	Rick Ryan
Direction	Malcolm MacPhail
Future	Lynn Wheeler

Great Wisdom From Small Sources

GLEN D. COLE

Part of the process of Jesus' life was that He "increased in wisdom and stature, and in favor with God and men" (Luke 2:52, NKJV). The follower of Jesus today should follow His example. The Bible is a great source of increased wisdom.

When someone says, "Please turn to Hebrews, chapter 11, in your Bibles," you know that you are about to be inspired by the "heroes of faith." But when someone says, "I am going to read to you some of the wisdom of Agur in Proverbs, chapter 30," you are apt to respond, "Who?" This little-known figure in the Old Testament introduces us to four small creatures in Proverbs 30:24-28 that will definitely help you gain wisdom for these last days.

Listed in order of their appearance, they are: the ant, the rock badger, the locust, and the spider (or lizard). The *Living Bible* says "lizard" . . . the Revised Standard Version says "lizard" . . . the Modern Language Version says "lizard." And since I like them better than spiders, we will also use the lizard as an example of wisdom.

ANTS: THE WISDOM OF PREPARATION

The New King James Bible reads this way: "The ants are a people not strong, yet they prepare their food in the summer" (Proverbs 30:25).

When my grandson Luke was about 6 years old, we could not locate him one evening as the sun was setting. Finally, we saw him across the street lying on the sidewalk with his face close to the cement. He would not respond to a call to come in, so I walked over to see what he was doing. I found him looking very closely at a group of ants that were hard at work preparing for colder weather. Luke was totally immersed in their effort to get ready for the future.

It is true; the ant works today for tomorrow! That is why Agur said, "They are exceedingly wise." Are you living in the past? Could you be harboring old hurts and wounds that should have been healed long ago? Wisdom that will build your Christian life and prepare you for the return of Jesus Christ demands that you drop that old weight and prepare for the future. The Bible says that "now is the accepted time" (2 Corinthians 6:2). If you are not wise, this season can be past you before you know it was here. The ant can carry off half of your picnic lunch if you don't watch out. While you are munching on your favorite food, ants can be carrying away other items as they use the summer to prepare for the winter that is ahead.

I have always been impressed with the story of Belshazzar in Daniel, chapter 5. As he was reveling in the greatest night of his career, with hundreds of guests and a magnificent orchestra, he was startled by some handwriting on the wall of his palace. It was not a long message. It was right to the point—"You are found wanting!" This king failed to use godly wisdom. He was defiling the sacred vessels of the temple in Jerusalem. What was to be his greatest night became his worst. The record states, "That very night Belshazzar, king of the Babylonians, was slain" (5:30, NIV). I don't believe he intended to leave the world that night. He was short on preparation. Very unwise!

The ant works in summer for the winter. He wants to be ready for what lies ahead. You could be approaching the winter season of your life. If so, stop today and learn wisdom from the ants in your neighborhood. I can guarantee you that they are wisely preparing for tomorrow.

THE ROCK BADGER: THE WISDOM OF TRUST

The second creature that Agur reminds us to study is the rock badger. My brief study of these little folks tells me they know how to hole up. Psalm 104:18 says, "The high hills are for the wild goats; the cliffs are a refuge for the rock badgers" (NKJV). They are about the size of rabbits but with smaller ears and shorter legs.

Agur tells us, "The rock badgers are a feeble folk, yet they make their homes in the crags" (Proverbs 30:26). Interesting that Scripture pictures them as "feeble folk." They are creatures of little power. So, what makes them so wise? They stick close to their security! If an eagle has an eye for one of these "feeble folk," it will have to knock down a mountain to get it. "They make their homes in the crags."

Where is your security? There is no doubt that true wisdom declares it to be in a living relationship with God. You can know "about God," you can even cite the Ten Commandments and the Apostles' Creed, but the only true security is in a daily relationship with the Lord. Notice these wisdom builders:

"The Lord is my rock and my fortress and my deliverer; my God, my strength, in whom I will trust" (Psalm 18:2).

"For by You I can run against a troop, by my God I can leap over a wall" (Psalm 18:29).

"Some trust in chariots, and some in horses; but we will remember the name of the Lord our God" (Psalm 20:7).

"The Lord is my light and my salvation" (Psalm 27:1).

If you have the wisdom of a rock badger, you *know* where you must be, and in *whom* you must trust. God's *increase of wisdom* warns us against the danger zones of life!

THE LOCUST: THE WISDOM OF UNITY

Now, what can the locust teach us about wisdom? If there is a threat to the church of Jesus Christ on earth today, I believe it to be the idea that you can be a Christian alone. The locust teams up with its friends and family members and becomes a threat to everyone. They can destroy entire communities just by hanging out together!

When do we become a threat to the devil? When we see ourselves as a body . . . a community of believers that remembers we are baptized into the company of others. The Exodus was not just for Moses. God said, "Let my people go!"

The *Sing His Praise* hymnbook included the great song "A Glorious Church" on page 558. If all of you reading this were with me right now, I would have you sing it out loud.

Do you hear them coming, brother,
Thronging up the steeps of light,
Clad in glorious shining garments,
Blood-washed garments pure and white?
'Tis a glorious Church without spot or wrinkle,
Washed in the blood of the Lamb;
'Tis a glorious Church, without spot or wrinkle,
Washed in the blood of the Lamb.

Another verse has the phrase "'Tis a grand, victorious army." I am stronger in my walk with God when I remember I am part of something far bigger, far stronger and far more secure than my weak self. The locust knows how to survive attack and storm—in strength of numbers. Be wise! Paul reminded the Galatians that "through love" they were to "serve one another" (Galatians 5:13). He reminded them that if they wanted to be strong and effective, they must not "bite and devour one another . . . lest [they] be consumed by one another" (verse 15).

A story in the March 1997 issue of *Pulpit Helps* (page 8) is worth remembering. "The Cats of Killkenny" is on the subject of "Unity."

The article speaks of a well-known limerick that conveys a message to all in the Lord's body. It is about two cats, each of which had an overrated opinion of itself. The arrogance of these two felines ultimately led to the demise of both.

> There once were two cats of Killkenny.
> Each thought there was one cat too many.
> They fought and they spit,
> They clawed and they bit,
> Till instead of two cats there weren't any!

The writer reminded every Christian that it is possible to see the saga of the Killkenny cats played out in the Lord's church with the same tragic results. An arrogant, self-righteous attitude displaying itself in religious bigotry is a shame upon our Prince of Peace who lived, died, and rose again that we all might be *one*. To be "top cat" is only to invite our own ultimate destruction. Paul did not succeed alone. Neither can we. May we have the increased wisdom of the locust that teaches us to hang together.

THE LIZARD: THE WISDOM OF FAITHFULNESS

There is yet one more friend mentioned. The lizard teaches us to keep on trying. This creature will find its way into a king's palace. Something as insignificant as a lizard can dwell with royalty. Have you ever said, "I am a nobody"? The wisdom of the lizard reminds us that there are no ordinary Christians, no ordinary people with God. He calls the nobodies of this world to follow Him. One day God will make us all like Jesus Christ!

I was ministering in the Philippines a number of years ago. Loving friends provided my wife and me a very nice room with all the amenities. However, we had not been there long until we became aware of other inhabitants. I looked up from our bed to see lizards darting here and there over wall and ceiling. My wife froze. How did they get in there? This room was for us! Well, they enjoyed our company. They evidently thought if these are special guests from the United States, we might as well enjoy the surroundings as well. So, there they were . . . all the while we were there! And if you try to catch a lizard you find out how sneaky fast they really are.

You may have picked up this book thinking there was no reason to keep going in your Christian walk. The lizard says, "Don't quit!" You must finish the race. You can be faithful. God will reward you even though you may think that your labor is in vain. It is not! Keep trying! "And let us not grow weary while doing good, for in due season we shall reap if we do not lose heart" (Galatians 6:9).

How grateful I am for the *increased wisdom* these four creatures have made available to me. They are very small. You can't even sit at their feet to learn because you probably couldn't find their feet. But their message is loud and clear . . . become wise! "He who has an ear, let him hear what the Spirit says" (Revelation 3:22).

Dr. Glen D. Cole served as superintendent of the Northern California and Nevada District Council of the Assemblies of God. Dr. Cole served some 17 years as senior pastor of Capital Christian Center in Sacramento, California, a 4,000-member congregation. He served on the Executive Presbytery of the General Council of the Assemblies of God for 10 years. He has been a member of the Foreign Missions Board and has served as the chairman of the Board of Directors for Central Bible College in Springfield, Missouri. He has ministered throughout the world at numerous conferences, district councils, camp meetings and churches. He has authored or co-authored numerous books and articles. A graduate of Central Bible College in Springfield, Missouri, he was awarded a doctor of divinity degree from Pacific Coast Bible College in Sacramento. He and his wife, Mary Ann, have two sons, who are also ministers, and seven grandchildren.

CHAPTER 12

The Holy Spirit's Presence

TERRY INMAN

A chilly wind and light snow hurried our task. We hastily hitched the Chevy truck to our retro project, a 20-foot vintage Airstream Camper Trailer. This aerodynamic chrome canister shines, even at age 40. My wife acquired this prized fixer-upper on an E-bay auction. Her brother and I reluctantly volunteered to rescue it from antiquity and tow it back to California. I'm sure the grandkids will love it.

We headed west, taking a less traveled road out of northern New Mexico with brief adventures at Monument Valley and the Grand Canyon. Our early morning panorama along the lonely two-lane highway was dry and desolate, scattered with occasional sagebrush, rocky bluffs, and the Native American dwellings of the Navahos.

We were delightfully surprised to learn that the real restoration project was two reluctant road-weary drivers. Authentic guy talk salted with amateur singing and frequent prayer helped the time fly by like the white lines in the center of the pavement. The chatter on board was substantive—not the usual work, sports, politics. We turned over the subterranean soil of the male soul. We were now softened, and open for what came next.

A THIRD PASSENGER

As we flew past a long dusty road, a bright orange poster tacked to an old fence post arrested our attention. The scribbled message read, "REVIVAL 6:30 PM." That's all it said—no people, no church anywhere, just a simple sign. It was more like a mirage in the desert. You would expect "No trespassing" or "No hunting" out here, but an invitation to "REVIVAL" was a bit extraordinary.

At that very moment, the lively Irish lyrics from recording artist Robin Mark's "Revival in Belfast" were being transmitted from the truck's CD player:

From the preacher preaching
when the well is dry,
to the lost soul reaching
for a higher high . . .
Revive us,
Revive us,
Revive us by your fire.[1]

Just moments later out in the middle of nowhere, both of us had an unusual awareness of a third Passenger. First it was my brother-in-law, a clinical psychologist, reporting spine tingling sensations and overwhelming joy. Then almost simultaneously I experienced a refreshing encounter. We both broke out in unashamed praise. We didn't attempt a jig!

This third Passenger has become quite familiar to me as the presence of the Holy Spirit.

In this chapter I hope to introduce you to our traveling companion in hopes that you will not only learn more about the third member of the Godhead but that you will also experience His presence in powerful new encounters of your own.

MORE THAN AN AIRSTREAM

In the Old Testament, God's Spirit is often identified by the Hebrew expression *ruach*, meaning "the wind" or "the breath."[2] The Holy Spirit is like a breath of fresh air. However, He is more than a reviving breeze. He is a powerful presence. He is a person.

King David understood and desired the personal presence of the Holy Spirit. As he repented of his sins and asked for restoration he pleaded, "Do not cast me from your presence or take your Holy Spirit from me" (Psalm 51:11).

The presence of the Holy Spirit attended many notable people of the Old Testament. They were accompanied and assisted by supernatural power to lead with courage, effect miracles and speak prophetically. Moses was so appreciative of the presence of the Holy Spirit, He expressed the hope that one day all God's people would be so endowed.[3]

Presence, more than an essence, is a tangible existence. It is being there, available and attentive, as opposed to absent. When we speak of a person's presence we are describing the whole of their personal qualities, their personality, or their individuality.

Each of us has his or her own unique sense of presence. Those around us experience our human attributes. In addition to our physical existence, we possess intelligence, emotions, and will. The Holy Spirit's identity is also defined by these same personal attributes.

He possesses intelligence; the Spirit knows the things of God (1 Corinthians 2:10,11). He has emotions; the Holy Spirit can be grieved (Ephesians 4:30). God's love flows to us through the Holy Spirit (Romans 15:30). He also exercises His will; the Spirit gives gifts to men as He wills (1 Corinthians 12:11). It's the "Spirit" part of His presence that mystifies us a bit. We can feel Him, even know Him, but we can't see Him or touch Him.

HOW DO YOU CONNECT WITH A GHOST?

Jesus promised the Holy Spirit's presence to His disciples who were feeling separation anxieties prior to His ascension. John records Jesus' assuring words: "And I will ask the Father, and he will give you another Counselor to be with you forever—the Spirit of truth. The world cannot accept him, because it neither sees him nor knows him. But you know him, for he lives with you and will be in you" (John 14:16,17).

"Counselor" is a good attempt to translate *parakletos*, the ancient Greek description Jesus used to promise the Spirit's presence.[4] The word clearly suggests nearness or closeness.

God the Father is someone with whom most of us can easily identify. "Father" is familiar. It's a human family title. Jesus Christ the Son of God also naturally generates endearment. We are sons and daughters; we can relate, especially to Jesus' incarnation. Jesus is God in human skin. But the Holy Spirit, or the Holy Ghost—how do you connect with a ghost?

It was my eighth birthday. I came home from school with one of those notes. I was struggling. The counsel from my dad was unusual. With his big warm hand on my shoulder he said, "Terry, you're 8 years old now. You need to be filled with the Holy Ghost. Tonight at the revival meeting I want you to seek your filling."

I was gloriously filled with God's Spirit. Speaking of "fillings," I lost my front baby tooth in the process. I was so overcome by the presence of the Holy Spirit that my loose tooth came out as the Holy Spirit was coming in! I was also given what the Scriptures call "new tongues."[5] I praised God in an unlearned language with a full heart and flowing tears of joy.

Admittedly the presence of the Holy Spirit can be somewhat intimidating to the novice. In fact, too many Christians simply pay little or no attention to the third identity of the Trinity, the Holy Spirit. Again and again in Revelation, the apostle John laments the fact that many ignore or reject Him. It's difficult for humankind to accept the Holy Spirit because He is unseen and unknown. But we can experience Him living with us, even in us.

God is getting closer than ever. He sent Jesus to be with us and die for us. He sends His Holy Spirit to be present in us. The Holy Spirit is not a thing, He is a supernatural being.

I questioned a missionary friend of mine why she always drops "the" as she addresses "Holy Spirit" with first person intimacy. She responded, "I don't say, 'The Jesus' when I talk to Him. Holy Spirit is also very personal to me. He is not *the* Holy Spirit, He is *my* Holy Spirit!" May I ask you, how present is God's gift to you?

COMPANY FOR THE JOURNEY

Modern technology has equipped some of our vehicles with guidance systems. Satellite-enabled audio and video mapping helps us get to our destination on time. Some of these systems include live support and roadside assistance. The Holy Spirit is our personal guidance system. He accompanies our spiritual journey. He is "live" help. He comes alongside to initiate and commence our pathway to eternity. He convicts, He purifies, He renews, He reveals, He guides, He leads, and He empowers us for life and service.

The Holy Spirit's influence is felt even in our pre-Christian experience. Jesus made it clear to His disciples that the Holy Spirit would be very present to persuade the world of its spiritual need. "When he comes, he'll expose the error of the godless world's view of sin, righteousness, and judgment: He'll show them that their refusal to believe in me is their basic sin; that righteousness comes from above, where I am with the Father, out of their sight and control; that judgment takes place as the ruler of this godless world is brought to trial and convicted" (John 16:8-11, *The Message*).

The Holy Spirit is also personally involved in our conversion. He guides us to Christ and renews us in Christ. John calls Him the Spirit of truth. "But when he, the Spirit of truth, comes, he will guide you into all truth. He will not speak on his own; he will speak only what he hears, and he will tell you what is yet to come. He will bring glory to me by taking from what is mine and making it known to you" (John 16:13,14, NIV).

The Holy Spirit is also intimately involved in our spiritual birth.[6] In addition, we are renewed by His presence.[7] This transformation is an ongoing result of His sanctifying presence.[8] As we partner with His presence a basketful of the Spirit's fruit is produced.

"But the fruit of the Spirit is love, joy, peace, patience, kindness, goodness, faithfulness, gentleness and self-control" (Galatians 5:22,23).

The Holy Spirit's presence in us is most tangible when those around us get a good taste.

We are enriched and equipped in every way by the presence of the Holy Spirit to live a promising and productive life.

GOING PLACES

The companionship of the Holy Spirit is so affirming, but He comes along for more than the ride. The Holy Spirit will take you places you never thought you would go. He empowers us to carry out God's purposes. Jesus mapped our destiny just before His departure from earth. His followers were wondering about the timing for a political takeover. He told them to hit the road.

"But you will receive power when the Holy Spirit comes on you; and you will be my witnesses in Jerusalem, and in all Judea and Samaria, and to the ends of the earth" (Acts 1:8).

The power of the Holy Spirit is on board to help spread the good news, one community, one nation, and one world at a time. This gift arrived on the Feast of Pentecost just 50 days after the Jewish Passover. The Holy Spirit's power came with special effects. The sound of wind, images of flames, and inspired praise in unlearned languages were like extraordinary road signs.[9]

Foreign pilgrims took the stories back to their nations. They heard the "witness" in their own dialects. The freshly filled apostle Peter was the first to pass along an explanation and extend the invitation. He made it prophetically clear that the power of the Holy Spirit is ours for the receiving.[10]

Don't leave home without it! Repent of any known sin. Receive total forgiveness. Immerse your life in Jesus Christ. Make it visible by baptism in water. Then just ask Jesus to saturate you with the Holy Spirit's presence and power.

As He fills you with His powerful presence, respond to the waves of love filling your being.[11] In childlike faith give voice to the Spirit-enabled articulations that the Scriptures encourage as "speaking in tongues."[12]

Make this part of your frequent prayer experience. This is not just an encounter; it is a journey. Stay filled with the presence of the Holy Spirit!

Terry Inman is senior pastor of Harbor Light Assembly of God in Fremont, California. This culturally diverse church in the heart of the San Francisco Bay Area averages 800 in attendance with more than 2,500 adherents and 1,400 in weekly small groups. The church operates two large preschools and a K-12 campus with more than 1,400 students.

Pastor Inman and his wife, Mary, have seven sons. Two are students at Evangel University and five are married. The Inmans enjoy their 11 grandchildren.

Pastor Inman provides leadership for a pastors' network in the region and travels frequently, equipping pastors and leaders, especially in unreached Third World nations. He serves as a general presbyter from the Northern California and Nevada District of the Assemblies of God.

In more than 35 years of ministry, Inman has served pastorates at Northfield Church in Gering, Nebraska; Church on the Hill in Vallejo, California; and at North Hollywood First Assembly of God. He is now serving in his 12th year at Harbor Light.

Inman has a passion for a "culturally relevant revival" that empowers transformed believers to reach the unchurched in the community and marketplace.

You may reach him at Terry@HarborLight.com.

.

CHAPTER 13

Transforming Your Life

RICK RYAN

We live in a society that promotes constant change, and much of that change is completely unnecessary. We remodel well-built homes just for a change of scenery. We undergo plastic surgery even when we are healthy and attractive. We replace clothes we have hardly worn in favor of new styles; we trade cars with low mileage for the current year's model; and we abandon computers, TVs, stereos, and other gadgets for larger screens, bigger sound, and a little more bling.

Yet, so many of us ignore our greatest need for change—a complete inner change, a transformation of the spirit.

Coming to Christ in faith is vital to that transformation. But even after we make that decision, God wants to continue His extreme transformation of our lives.

Our spiritual composition determines what we are made of in times of crisis or in quiet times, when no one is watching and when everyone is watching. Our spiritual identity is the truest part of who we are. Strip away surface personality, your position in your community, and whatever title you have on the job. You're left with your character, your deepest emotional makeup that energizes and shapes how you interact with others.

That is the part of you God wants to transform. Just imagine what could happen to you and for you if you stepped back and invited the Holy Spirit to fully accomplish all of the inner change He desires to bring about in your life.

"For those God foreknew he also predestined to be conformed to the likeness of his Son, that he might be the firstborn among many brothers" (Romans 8:29, NIV).

That's the real focus behind the concept of this book. *Jesus and you* should describe every part of your life. At home, at church, on the job, in your car, on vacation, in your easy chair—wherever you are and whatever you are doing, God is still working in you to make you more like His Son. The only question is, are you allowing the details of life to create barriers to that process, or are you committing all of your life to God and allowing Him to use each moment to contribute to the transformation He desires.

THE PROCESS OF TRANSFORMATION

Our society calls for constant, often shallow, change. And it demands that change in a moment. Sometimes that mindset finds its way into our walk of faith. We recognize areas in our lives that need change. But we want God to do it in an instant. The Christian life is a long, sometimes difficult, maturation process.

God's process of transformation will address the long-term commitments you make. Ask yourself what you give your time to and where most of your focus is directed. God's transforming work will help you see those commitments as subject to His lordship and needing His approval and blessing.

"Whatever you do, whether in word or deed, do it all in the name of the Lord Jesus, giving thanks to God the Father through him" (Colossians 3:17).

God's process of transformation will address the weak areas in your life. He will invite you to strengthen your commitment to spiritual disciplines such as prayer and Scripture study and fasting. He will call on you to put aside compromising habits and worldly attitudes.

"Let us throw off everything that hinders and the sin that so easily entangles, and let us run with perseverance the race marked out for us" (Hebrews 12:1).

God's process of transformation will keep you focused on the present and hoping in the future rather than dwelling in the past. You will discover that each day is a new opportunity to accomplish something of eternal value for the Kingdom.

"Forgetting what is behind and straining toward what is ahead, I press on toward the goal to win the prize for which God has called me heavenward in Christ Jesus" (Philippians 3:13,14).

THREE TRANSFORMING TRUTHS

As each of the above Scriptures illustrates, you are intimately involved in this process of spiritual transformation. *Your* words and deeds are to reflect the character of Christ (Colossians 3:17). *You* are running with perseverance (Hebrews 12:1). *You* are to press toward heaven's goal (Philippians 3:13,14). But never forget, God is at work in your life to make it possible for you to live for Him. It is *His* plan that *He* is bringing to reality in you.

"'For I know the plans I have for you,' declares the Lord, 'plans to prosper you and not to harm you, plans to give you hope and a future. Then you will call upon me and come and pray to me, and I will listen to you. You will seek me and find me when you seek me with all your heart'" (Jeremiah 29:11-13).

Once you have in focus that God is divinely at work in you, and you are to actively respond to Him, you discover three transforming truths.

God will speak to your heart by His Holy Spirit. God's communication to your spirit from His Spirit is so personal, so direct. Yes, He will use other believers to speak truth into your life, but He desires an intimacy with you that is as unique as you are. The Holy Spirit will guide you daily and directly.

"Whether you turn to the right or to the left, your ears will hear a voice behind you, saying, 'This is the way; walk in it'" (Isaiah 30:21).

God will expose the counterfeit controls in your life and help you overcome them. As you listen to the Holy Spirit and begin to view your circumstances through His holy gaze, you will not as readily give in to the influences in life that would tell you that you can't, you won't, or that something is impossible.

God has not called you to a life of defeat or to be hemmed in by failure-imposed boundaries. The ultimate fulfillment of His plan for you is as big as eternity. And so much of that plan begins today right where you are.

"In all these things we are more than conquerors through him who loved us. For I am convinced that neither death nor life, neither angels nor demons, neither the present nor the future, nor any powers, neither height nor depth, nor anything else in all creation, will be able to separate us from the love of God that is in Christ Jesus our Lord" (Romans 8:37-39).

God will replace your self-deception with His truth. Even followers of Christ may at times listen more closely to their own human understanding than to the divine wisdom of God's Spirit. The process of spiritual transformation calls for a transition from self-focus to self-surrender.

There are times you can be self-deceived and think you can respond to God's commands and His calling through your flesh. You believe that somehow if you work hard enough, God will be impressed by your human effort and will bless you on the strength of your personal merit.

Such self-deception leads only to despair. In time, some believers who become focused on their own flawed attempts at righteousness and obedience give up the fight for truth and surrender to depression. They close themselves off from God's Word and His transformation.

But what happens when you surrender to God and obey Him through the transforming power of the Holy Spirit at work within you?

Take a look at Paul the apostle's detailed description of that process in Romans 8. So often, we like to glance at Romans 8:28 and summarize our entire walk of faith in that one verse. "Everything has to turn out all right," we tell ourselves, "because God is making it happen that way."

But Paul goes so much further than that synopsis of God's work in our lives. In rich detail, he points us to the constant work of the Spirit in us that allows us to overcome temptation and live victoriously and productively for the Kingdom.

INVITATION FOR TRANSFORMATION

What's holding you back? Why not press forward and invite God to make your life into a new and powerful daily experience. It's a process that begins with your simple invitation, just like at salvation. Pray this prayer:

Heavenly Father, help me to relax in my spirit and hear Your Spirit's voice in my soul. I am renouncing the influences I have allowed to control my life, with the confidence that You are willing to lovingly guide me in all things. I want You, Jesus, and Your Word alone to inspire me. I am tired of the self-deception that has chained me and limited Your fullness in me. I am convinced that You are an infinitely greater force within me than the prince of this world who seeks to destroy me. I yield my life completely to You. Be Lord of all!

You can feel the change within even as you whisper this prayer, can't you? It is God's Holy Spirit working on your behalf in you and for you. You are experiencing just what Jesus promised His disciples. Jesus assured them that the ministry of the Holy Spirit in their lives would be so powerful and effective that they would be blessed even more than they had when Jesus was with them on earth (John 16:7).

That's an amazing truth to ponder. Just think, as you surrender to the Holy Spirit's influence, He is at work in you in a more direct and powerful manner than anything the disciples experienced during Jesus' earthly ministry.

Now live in it, act on it, and make this extreme transformation eternal. Meditate on what Roy Lessin writes:

You are the *Lord's*!
You are in God's place at God's *perfect* time!
Your days are in His hands, and He is your *future*!
He has gifted you and placed His hand upon you to *bless you* and make you a blessing!
The burden of your ministry is not yours to carry—
As you *rest*, He will work;
As you abide, He will bring fruit;
As you sow, He will give the *increase*!
He is your shield and your exceeding great reward![1]

Rick and Denise Ryan serve as lead pastors of Orange County Worship Center (www.ocwc.org) in Santa Ana, California. Rick has been a youth pastor in Washington and California, the district Chi Alpha director for Arizona, the southwest regional Chi Alpha representative, the district youth and Christian education director for the Arizona District, a missionary in Costa Rica (where Theo and Giselle, their children, were born), and a missionary with the Book of Hope. Before pastoring in Santa Ana, Rick and Denise were the lead pastors at Sequoyah Community Church in Oakland, California.

CHAPTER 14

Finding Guidance From God in Difficult Times

MALCOLM MACPHAIL

I was playing a round of golf in Monterey, California, on a warm spring day on May 19, 1994. I was in Monterey to meet with a representative from Fellowship of Christian Athletes and discuss plans for a golf camp to reach out to students in the area. The morning was progressing well, when I began to feel pain in my abdomen. As the pain continued, my partner became convinced I had developed a hernia. Upon finishing the round, I called my wife and shared this concern with her.

Every day I make it a habit to read the Book of Proverbs. Little did I know that Proverbs 27:1—"Do not boast about tomorrow, for you do not know what a day may bring forth" (NIV)—would come true for me.

I thought my routine examination and blood test would confirm the hernia. Instead, four doctors began to ask a series of questions.

"Have you been tired lately?"

I had. I was a husband and father of four young children (8, 6, 4, and 2). I coached two soccer teams, pastored a growing church, and served as volunteer chaplain of the Gilroy Police Department.

"Have you noticed any weight loss?"

Sure, but I was feeling good about it.

"Mr. MacPhail," they continued, "your blood test confirms you have an adult form of leukemia—Chronic Myelogenous Leukemia (CML)."

Leukemia is a cancer that affects the white blood cells (the immune system). CML produces immature white blood cells that are not capable of fighting off disease. The disease has a life span of 2-3 years. In 1994 there was no cure other than a bone marrow transplant. Doctors believed I could never have a transplant as I had no matching relatives. Without a transplant the disease accelerates and takes over the body.

My wife sat in shock after the consultation. I went to her and from deep in my spirit came these words: "Kathy, this sickness is not unto death, but that the works of God would be glorified." Jesus spoke words like these in John 11:4. And Jesus would walk with us through the process of giving glory to God.

Let me share some spiritual principles.

WHEN YOU NEED DIRECTION, YOUR DECISION SHOULD BRING GLORY TO GOD

Right there in the hospital office we dedicated ourselves in prayer that during this ordeal everything we did would glorify the God we serve. We began to get a glimpse of the truth that prevails throughout Scripture—that the testing of our faith through sickness, disease, difficult relationships, family, marriage, finances, and more are all meant to ultimately bring glory to the God we serve. This principle would guide us in the tough times of decision-making.

Without the possibility of a bone marrow transplant, we began some experimental forms of chemotherapy. This made me very sick. Many of our friends and family held us up in prayer and support. We began to hear from loved ones who had been praying and asking God for a miracle in my life. Some called and shared Scriptures that the Holy Spirit had directed them to as they had prayed for me. We noticed that those Scriptures were also some of the same words that we were hearing from the Lord and holding onto through the process of making decisions about medicines and therapies.

This is where we learned the second principle:

GOD'S WORD WILL GUIDE YOU THROUGH THE PROCESS
(See Psalm 119:49,50,105.)

These words from Scripture became our foundation as we had to make ever-more-difficult decisions. My blood was tested three times a week to monitor what the chemo was doing to my other blood components. Each time it would come back with the cancerous cells. Twice a year we would have bone marrow biopsies and they also would come back with no change to the cancer. We would get discouraged that God had not healed me or that there seemed to be no answers or possible cure.

But we discovered a third principle:

ALWAYS REMEMBER THAT YOU CAN BELIEVE THE DIAGNOSIS . . . BUT THE PROGNOSIS IS IN THE HANDS OF GOD
(See Luke 18:27.)

This principle brought us hope as time passed and we didn't see any results and I still had cancer in my body. We, with our church family and loved ones, continued to pray for a miracle.

Possibilities began to surface. One of my doctors at Stanford Medical Center submitted my name to the National Marrow Donor Program to begin a worldwide search for a possible bone marrow match from an unrelated donor. The best odds for a bone marrow transplant are from a sibling. My only sibling was born from a different father and even if there was a slight chance of him matching, I had not seen him in more than 20 years and had no idea where he was. Time was passing and the search was proving futile.

Yet, we continued to pray.

About four years into this process we received a crushing report. DNA tests showed that I had a rare gene. My odds of finding a perfect match were impossible. We could have the transplant with an imperfect match, but were given only a 30 percent chance of survival, and Stanford would not do the transplant.

"Go home and enjoy what time you have left," we were told.

We were stunned, discouraged, and afraid. Yet we turned again to the Lord for direction. We needed to decide what to do next. I had been searching for other options as we prayed for the next step. We found a research center in the state of Washington that would interview me to see if I qualified for a transplant. Kathy and I flew up to the Fred Hutchinson Cancer Research Center in Seattle and sat with the doctors.

This is where principle number four comes in:

YOUR PRAYERS AND SUBSEQUENT HEARING FROM GOD WILL GUIDE YOUR DECISION
(See Psalm 17:6 and Hebrews 3:7.)

The doctors said they would do the transplant, but my odds of survival would only be 30 percent and there could be complications from rejection. Kathy and I prayed. We both felt that everything the Lord had done and all the prayer and Scripture we had received had led us to this point. We went ahead with the transplant.

We were full of faith and we were also afraid. I asked God for courage. A quote that has been special to me is, "Courage is not the absence of fear, but the ability to move forward despite it." We moved forward, confident God would see us through.

Kathy and I moved to Seattle with our four children in January 1999 full of faith, hope, and confidence in God and the support and prayers of our family, friends, and community. An unrelated donor had been located and the process of the transplant would begin in 30 days.

With a 30 percent chance of survival, I had to prepare my wife and children for every possibility. Wills and DNR[1] statements had to be readied. I wrote a life manual for each of my children and spent personal days with them to prepare them for all that would take place. Whether God chose to take me home or leave me on earth for the remainder of my days was in His hands. My children needed to know that.

"The servant of the Lord is indestructible until God is through with him," I assured my family. Isn't that true for all of us? The Psalmist David said, "My times are in your hands" (Psalm 31:15). Our trust was in God's plan.

A week before the March 5 transplant, I entered the hospital for two days of lethal dosages of chemotherapy and five days of full body radiation. They had to destroy all my current bone marrow and the leukemia in my body before the donor's bone marrow could be transfused.

On Day "0" the donor's marrow arrived in an ice chest from Charleston, S.C., and was infused into my body. Our family and friends rejoiced in the new life that was coming into my body and the fact that at that time, after almost five years, I was finally cancer free.

But another battle was just beginning. Over the next 45 days I would battle through skin and liver complications. Massive amounts of anti-rejection drugs were administered. During this time much prayer was offered from our family and community. Through good medicine and much prayer we survived this latest battle. After 100 days doctors gave us the green light to return home to California.

I resumed my long-term care with Stanford Medical Center and was confined to my home (I called it house arrest) for the next six months with as little personal contact as possible. I loved being a pastor and longed to return to the ministry. The transplant was successful and I longed to get back to normalcy.

But I learned a final principle:

THE THIRD PERSON OF THE TRINITY, THE HOLY SPIRIT, WILL CONFIRM WITH YOUR SPIRIT THAT THE DECISION OF THE LORD HAS BEEN ACCOMPLISHED

After five years battling cancer and then a year of transplant and recovery, I am thankful for God's confirmation and confidence at every step of the way. The decisions we made would never have been possible without God's Word being our foundation of faith and confidence for each step of the way.

Proverbs 16:9 says, "In his heart a man plans his course, but the Lord determines his steps." The prayers of my wife and family, church and community were a constant source of encouragement. These principles helped us navigate through the tough decisions we faced.

I truly believe that these principles will guide you through your test—whether it be a life-threatening health issue, or a marriage that is failing, or a rebellious child who is bringing pain in your life. May I encourage you to walk close to Jesus and apply the principles of God's Word to whatever test you may be facing? To trust and believe that God might just have a miracle in store for your life?

For me, the words of the Psalmist continue to ring true: "I am still confident of this: I will see the goodness of the Lord in the land of the living. Wait for the Lord; be strong and take heart and wait for the Lord" (Psalm 27:13,14, NIV).

Malcolm MacPhail is the senior pastor of New Hope Community Church in Gilroy, California, and has been serving the church and community of Gilroy for more than 14 years. He has been married to his wife, Kathy, for 22 years and they have four children: Danny, 20; Jeff, 18; Ryan, 16; and Alexis, 14.

MacPhail was born in Chicago and raised in San Francisco and San Bruno, California. After hearing God's call on his life, he went to Capital Bible Institute in Sacramento, California, where he received a degree in pastoral ministries. He served as a youth pastor at Capital Christian Center in Sacramento under Pastor Glen Cole, and again at Bethel Church in Modesto under Pastor Cliff Traub. He then pioneered a singles ministry in Santa Rosa under Pastor John Warren Jr. before coming to New Hope in Gilroy in 1992, at the age of 33. Pastor MacPhail has been serving in ministry for more than 22 years. He also serves as the police and fire chaplain in Gilroy.

MacPhail's passion and vision is that New Hope Community Church be a church that "reaches the unchurched and assimilates them into a Spirit-filled body of believers." He has traveled overseas, primarily to Southeast Asia, training leaders and teaching and preaching. Malcolm loves golf, sports with his children, movies with his daughter, and getaways with his wife. Everything he does is meant to "expand the kingdom of God."

CHAPTER 15

Leaving the Past Behind

LYNN WHEELER

Most of us have been there. You wake up and your alarm clock is flashing off and on. It is 7 a.m., but the clock is flashing 3:30 a.m. You needed to be up at 6 a.m. Because of a power failure in the night, you were stuck in the past. Now your day has been altered and you will spend most of your morning catching up.

STUCK IN THE PAST

Many of God's people are stuck in the past because of a spiritual power failure. They experience constant flashbacks of past sins, mistakes, and bad decisions. This isn't just a habit of our own minds. The enemy of our souls constantly reminds us of our past failures.

I want to remind every child of God that the devil is a liar! The Bible clearly states, "When he [the devil] lies, he speaks his native language, for he is a liar and the father of lies" (John 8:44, NIV). The first recorded conversation the devil ever had was filled with lies. In Genesis 3:4 he said to Eve, "You will not surely die." That was a lie—a direct contradiction of what God had said.

I do not like being lied to. Lies and deception are some of the most destructive emotional forces in life.

I'll admit, not every untruth I've encountered has been deadly. One or two have even made me laugh. One day I was sitting in algebra class in high school and our teacher, Mr. Bonds, was trying to explain an a + b = c formula. No one was getting it. He noticed the confusion and boredom on our faces. He put down his chalk and proceeded to give a lengthy speech on the importance of algebra and why we needed to pay attention.

In the course of that speech he said, "Students, you must pay attention because some day in your life, you will need this." He lied. After that class, I never used it again except, of course, for a sermon illustration.

Did your dentist ever lie to you? "This won't hurt at all," he says, then sticks a drill in your mouth and *it hurts.*

What about road signs? They sometimes lie too. Did you ever see the sign that says "MEN WORKING" and they're not? "Watch for ice on bridge"? In Texas . . . in July?

Other lies are not funny at all. Like the time someone pretended to be something to you that they were not. Like the lies that were told to you that cost you time, money, or even years of your life. Many people are living with the painful effects of being lied to in the past. Without God's help, those effects will never go away. These are the lies that cause us to agree with the biblical writer who said, "My tears have been my food day and night" (Psalm 42:3).

Satan's lies about our past can cripple us if we let them. Always remember, the enemy's constant reminders of our past are null and void. The devil's words have no credibility. He cannot be trusted. You are a child of God and the devil does not have permission to speak into your life. He is a liar! He can never change the abiding truth of God in your life.

RELIVING BAD CHOICES

Our past mistakes have been created by our bad decisions. We have all used poor judgment at times, resulting in bad decisions that cause us to live with the consequences. These are the mistakes that the enemy capitalizes on with great intensity. At times, the devil's reminders create a guilt that seems unbearable. The devil never fights fair.

This attack often comes when our relationship with God seems solid. Our prayer life is a regular part of our day. We feel as though we are growing in God and in His Word.

Then the devil attacks our spirit. He dredges up memories of things we did wrong—sins that are under the blood of Jesus, but still resident in our memory. Satan begins to speak to us. The devil starts saying things like, "Look what you did" or "You can never be forgiven" or "You call yourself a Christian after all the bad things you have done?" He tries to fill our hearts and minds with doubt and guilt. John 10:10 says, "The thief comes only to steal and kill and destroy."

Sometimes we try to deny Satan's influence. "He can't speak to me since I'm a follower of Christ," we tell ourselves. Remember, Satan even tempted Jesus (Matthew 4:1-11). If the devil could speak his lies to the Son of God, he can inject his hellish thoughts into the mind of God's follower. But that does not mean Satan has power over the believer.

Remember, child of God, you are forgiven and you are free! The Bible says, "There is therefore now no condemnation to those who are in Christ Jesus, who do not walk according to the flesh, but according to the Spirit. For the law of the Spirit of life in Christ Jesus has made me free from the law of sin and death" (Romans 8:1,2, NKJV).

Yes, John 10:10 reminds us, the devil is a thief who would try to steal and kill and destroy all that God is accomplishing in us. But the rest of John 10:10 says, "I have come that they may have life, and have it to the full" (NIV).

CALLED TO THE FUTURE

Child of God, you cannot move into your spiritual future looking in the rearview mirror. Paul wrote in Philippians

3:13,14, "Brothers, I do not consider myself yet to have taken hold of it. But one thing I do: Forgetting what is behind and straining toward what is ahead, I press on toward the goal to win the prize for which God has called me heavenward in Christ Jesus."

Tear down that spiritual rearview mirror! Forget what is behind! Keep pressing toward the prize!

Your future is bright. "'For I know the plans I have for you,' declares the Lord, 'plans to prosper you and not to harm you, plans to give you hope and a future" (Jeremiah 29:11). Your best days are ahead of you. Let the past be past. If you are going to be effective for God, your past cannot have a future and your future cannot have a past.

One of the worst things about living in the past is that it paralyzes our future. God's goal is to get you where He wants you to be. The devil's goal is to paralyze you right where you are. One of the ways Satan does that is to constantly bring up your past. Shake off those memories of failure and step into what God has for you.

I have heard many preachers say it this way: "When the devil reminds you of your past, you remind him of his future." Revelation 20:10 describes the end result of the devil: "The devil, who deceived them, was thrown into the lake of burning sulfur, where the beast and the false prophet had been thrown. They will be tormented day and night for ever and ever."

Do not allow a spiritual power outage to cause you to be stuck in the past. Stay plugged into the mercy of God that never runs dry. The Lord would say to you as He said to the apostle Paul in 2 Corinthians 12:9, "My grace is sufficient for you, for my power is made perfect in weakness." Paul went on to say in the same verse, "Therefore I will boast all the more gladly about my weaknesses, so that Christ's power may rest on me." Even when we are weak and feel like we cannot get "plugged back in to God," His grace connects us. His mercy endures forever.

After struggling with memories of my past for more than a decade, one day I had one of those defining, refreshing moments with God. He spoke these words into my spirit: *Position your past and pursue your future!*

May I encourage you to do the same? *Position your past.* That is what it is—your past! Position it there and leave it there. You cannot unscramble eggs and you cannot go back one second in time. So, position your past behind you and never allow it to come forward again.

Also, *pursue your future.* Remember, you are forgiven and you are free. Your best days are ahead. Go for it. May God give you spiritual amnesia regarding your past. Hold your head up high; you are a child of God, an eternal heir of your Heavenly Father, a co-heir with Jesus Christ himself (Romans 8:17). Heaven's royal blood is flowing through your veins!

Lynn Wheeler has been traveling domestically and internationally for more than 20 years preaching the gospel. He has spoken at camps, conventions, retreats, and crusades all over the nation as well as in South America, Russia, Ukraine, Romania, and Ireland. He is a 1982 graduate of Central Bible College in Springfield, Missouri. He also spent four years as youth pastor at Crossroads Cathedral in Oklahoma City, Oklahoma.

Lynn and his wife, Dianna, have three children and reside in Greenbrier, Arkansas.

Section

4

"Those who become a defense for the defenseless invoke God's favor on their families, their work, their health, and more."

—Huldah Buntain

Compassion	Huldah Buntain
Family	Beth Grant
Finances	Pete Vossler
Blessings	Aaron Fruh
Evangelism	Mark Elliott

CHAPTER 16

Four Hallmarks of Christ's Compassion

HULDAH BUNTAIN

Compassion for people in need was a priority for Christ during His ministry on earth. As the body of Christ, Christians are to communicate Jesus' love and compassion to a lost and hurting world today. Much of my life has been committed to touching the hurting multitudes of India.

In a land of more than a billion people, the need is staggering. Calcutta, our center of operations for many years, by itself represents 18 million people, most of whom live in overcrowded poverty.

When we look at the massive scale of the world's needs, we may be tempted to give up. "What difference can I make?" we ask. Jesus gave us four simple principles that can energize our compassion for others.

PRIORITIZE THE PERSON

Often we think about ministry in terms of a "lost soul." Jesus did not see a person's soul in isolation.

"Love the Lord your God with all your heart and with all your soul and with all your mind and with all your strength," Jesus said in Mark 12:30 (NIV). Jesus saw a whole person whose entire existence needed a healing relationship with His Father.

When my husband, Mark, and I first ministered in India we would hold tent meetings, and Mark preached messages that drew many to salvation. But during one service, an elderly beggar ran to the front and began waving his finger at Mark. "Preacher," he said, "feed our bellies and then you can tell us there's a God in heaven that loves us."

That interruption greatly affected our ministry. We discovered that a bowl of rice, a warm bed, a human touch and a kind word given in the name of Jesus could be the difference between physical and spiritual death. Great needs can persist after a person responds to compassion and makes a decision for Christ. We must take the long view of far-reaching needs.

One afternoon a young woman burst into my office, tears streaming down her face. "You say I should leave prostitution, but how do I feed my kids?" she asked bluntly. She had turned her life over to Christ, and she knew she should no longer sell her body—but her children needed to eat. She didn't have any skills, so how would she survive?

"What can I do?" she repeated.

"God has a plan and purpose for your life," I said. "Trust in Him and He will direct your paths."

"But how does that help me this moment?" she asked.

I prayed silently, asking the Lord for the right words. "I'll tell you what God wants you to do," I said, "and what He wants me to do. Do you have a Bible?"

"Yes," she said in a disappointed tone.

"I want you to read that Bible and pray every day that God will give you a job. In the meantime, I'll personally support you and your family. I want you to come in tomorrow and we will begin looking for a new occupation for you." A smile exploded onto her face, followed by tears. She had only known abuse and neglect. Now someone was showing her true love and concern.

Jesus made time for everyone who wanted a life change. He

invested himself in those He came to save. Today we must be willing to invest ourselves in the salvation—both spiritual and physical—of men, women, and children around the world.

DEFEND THE DEFENSELESS

Without Christ, people are defenseless against Satan's attacks and the many expressions of sin in this fallen world. God's Word commands us to defend the defenseless, to be charitable to the less fortunate. Those who become a defense for the defenseless invoke God's favor on their families, their work, their health, and more. Psalm 82:3,4 says, "Defend the cause of the weak and fatherless; maintain the rights of the poor and oppressed. Rescue the weak and needy; deliver them from the hand of the wicked."

During a regional conflict in India years ago, many men and women were dying bloody deaths. I knew many children were being orphaned. These small victims wandered through the villages and cities. Their parents' deaths were sudden; theirs were slow and agonizing.

If only we could get more of them to the Calcutta Mercy orphanage there, I said to myself, *it would be a place of refuge where they'd receive nutritious meals, clothing, and shelter.*

God began to open doors to reach out to these war orphans. Pastor John Khuma, the director of the home, eventually oversaw the addition of dormitories, a Bible college, and a school. That orphanage's ministry team became a living example of James 1:27: "Religion that God our Father accepts as pure and faultless is this: to look after orphans and widows in their distress and to keep oneself from being polluted by the world."

Few people are more defenseless than a blind child. In India particularly, the blind are often neglected and even viewed as a curse. For years we had wanted to start a ministry to the blind, but the right doors had not opened. One day a man came to my office. He and his wife had taken seven blind children into their home. I agreed to visit his home the following day.

"These are our children," the man said proudly, pointing to seven children simultaneously engaged in some sort of learning activity. Some were reading Braille books; others were listening to music; another was learning how to wash his face and hands. They giggled and played unlike any blind children I had seen in India.

We decided to partner with this couple and start a ministry. After several months of searching, God led us to a perfect piece of land. Today, there is a school complete with dormitories and a chapel. The children are educated with Braille curriculum and audiotapes. Numbers of children have also had their sight restored thanks to surgeries by our doctors at our Calcutta Mercy Hospital.

VALUE THE ONE

Jesus offered His life for a lost world. But throughout His earthly ministry, He touched individual lives. The need around the world is staggering and overwhelming. But God asks us to simply respond when He puts someone in our path who needs our help. Our response may mean the difference between life and death—here on earth and in eternity.

I remember a mother who came to my home in the middle of the night. As she unraveled the story of her dying son's kidney disorder my heart went out to her.

"Where is your son?"

"In the emergency room at your hospital."

The first stop of my day was the boy's hospital room. His thin face was ashen. Beads of sweat had formed on his head. His heavy breathing was enough to tell me death was near.

"I've seen many sick people, but this boy's kidneys are so far gone he will die shortly," one of our doctors whispered to me. "Barring a divine touch, I don't think he is going to make it."

I responded with a prayer: "In Jesus' name, I ask that You heal this boy as a testimony of Your glory."

The next morning the doctor gave me the news: "He is

slightly better, but he will not live if he does not have a kidney transplant. It is not a procedure we can do here; he'll have to see a specialist at a larger hospital."

"Then that is what we will have to do," I said.

"A transplant of this kind costs at least $20,000," the doctor said.

"God will provide it," I said. "Please make arrangements."

My instructions surprised even me, but the boy's sickness rested heavily on my heart. *How could I not do everything in my power to help a mother help her son?*

God worked two miracles. A minister from the United States heard of the boy's need and paid for his surgery. Then God provided a donor in the boy's family with a suitable kidney. The transplant took place and the boy made a remarkable comeback. Today that boy, his mother, and their entire family are serving the Lord.

Some might ask why we would go to such lengths to rescue one boy, to save one life. But Jesus did that for us. He touched the world by ministering to every person the Father placed in His path. He healed the leper, touched the blind man, gave spiritual guidance to the prostitute, forgave the tax collector, healed the crippled man. He brought hope to the world one person at a time.

INVEST AND MULTIPLY

When we follow the Holy Spirit's leading, as Jesus did, and touch individual lives with gospel-motivated compassion, a divine multiplication goes into effect. The Book of Acts gives powerful illustrations of this principle. We read of Christ building His church as His disciples obediently ministered to a cripple, an Ethiopian, a businesswoman and a jailer among others.

The power of one is staggering, but we have to see that power with heaven's vision. I remember one little boy who seemed to appear from nowhere at my office. His body was rail thin, his dark skin covered in a layer of grime and his hair unkempt. The rags that clung to his body were soiled and torn. But his bright eyes and wide smile were like magnets pulling me closer to him.

"I want to go to school," he said, raising his chin proudly.

"Will you be a good student?" I asked.

He nodded, and his big eyes lit up even more.

"Do you promise to work hard every day?"

"I will do my best," he promised.

He excelled in his studies. Eating regularly made him physically healthy. Studying God's Word made him spiritually strong. After graduating from high school, he proceeded to college and on to medical school. Today, he is one of the physicians in the Mission hospital, touching thousands of lives.

Once, as I waited to board a plane, another young man approached me. "You don't remember me, do you?" he asked.

I looked up from the book on my lap and studied his face. "I'm not sure," I said.

"When I was a little boy, I attended your school. You gave me an education. You gave me God."

"Thank you for your kind words," I said, smiling. "Where are you now?"

"I live in Florida. I manage a large company there. My life is far beyond anything I dreamed as a boy. Not only has God given me a hope for my future here on earth, but He has given me a hope for eternity. I'm doing everything I can to follow your example and help other children."

God has allowed me to accomplish more than I ever thought possible. I'll never stop thanking Him for the privilege of showing so many poor and needy the path to a better life. India's needs—as well as the needs of the world at large—will always tug at my heart and threaten to overwhelm my senses. If believers will apply these four hallmarks of Jesus' compassion, God will continue to maximize His work despite our limitations.

Dr. Huldah Buntain founded Calcutta Mercy Ministries with her daughter, Bonnie Buntain-Long, in 2005. CMM is the latest development of a ministry begun and expanded by Mark and Huldah Buntain since they first ministered in India in 1954. Mark Buntain tirelessly served the poor of India until his death in 1989.

Buntain ministry milestones include an English medium school established in 1964 with 200 poor children, a daily feeding program begun in 1965, the establishment of a medical clinic in 1971, the construction of a hospital from 1975-1977, a school of nursing opened in 1979 and a cardiac care facility inaugurated by Mother Teresa in 1992. Each of these ministries has continued to expand and diversify, now reaching 11 states in India.

From 1994-2005, Dr. Buntain saw the work in Calcutta grow to include more than 700 churches, 80 schools with more than 30,000 children, expanded programs in the teacher's training college and the school of nursing, a children's home, rural medical clinics and a daily feeding program for more than 18,000 people. Calcutta Mercy Hospital serves more than 100,000 patients a year.

You may reach Dr. Buntain's ministry at info@buntain.org (web site: www.buntain.org).

Your Family Serving God

BETH GRANT

Our two young daughters were sitting at the kitchen table after school engrossed in serious conversation. As a missionary family, we were frequently separated from my husband during the school year as he traveled in ministry, and our youngest daughter, Jennifer, had reached her limit of missing her daddy.

"Mommy, why does Daddy have to travel *so much*?" she asked.

Before I could speak, her older, wiser sister, Rebecca, injected a quick response that she had heard many times. "Jennifer, you know God has called Daddy to preach and he needs to travel to do it!"

But her little sister was undeterred. "Yes, I know that! *But does God make his schedule?!*"

Our 5-year-old daughter captured what we adults often forget. As followers of Jesus, our relationship with Him should shape and define every area of our lives—even the way we prioritize our time. While Western culture has traditionally divided the world between the spiritual and secular, God's Word and the life of Jesus Christ challenge believers to an integrated life of faith. In no area is this integration of faith and life more strategic, strengthening, and potentially life-changing than in our homes.

The Old Testament Book of Deuteronomy articulates this day-to-day integration of faith in God with the daily life events of our families in Moses' instructions to God's people in Deuteronomy 6:5-9 (NIV):

"Love the Lord your God with all your heart and with all your soul and with all your strength. These commandments that I give you today are to be upon your hearts. Impress them on your children. Talk about them when you sit at home and when you walk along the road, when you lie down and when you get up. Tie them as symbols on your hands and bind them on your foreheads. Write them on the doorframes of your houses and on your gates."

This integrated approach to our family serving God is in great contrast to one in which our relationship to God is reserved for Sunday morning church attendance. Rather, our faith in God and serving Him with all of our hearts become the unifying threads through the course of our family's days. Faith and service form a framework by which we make decisions, relate to others, and relate to our world. But how do we go about bringing the love and life of Jesus into the very heart of our family life?

INVITE YOUR FAMILY BY WORD AND DEED TO FOLLOW YOU AS YOU FOLLOW JESUS

Images speak powerfully to me in my personal journey of faith. Similarly, I have found images have been very helpful in learning to weave faith in God and His life-changing truth into the fabric of our family's life and relationships. One of the images that has guided my responses to life and its events has been my commitment to our daughters to model what it means to follow Jesus. In my mind, I am always holding on to the hand of Jesus to follow Him with one hand and holding on to the hands of our daughters who follow behind me with the other. Jesus is leading me, and I am leading them while together we follow Him.

In a practical sense, Christian parenting is first and foremost mentoring our children to follow Jesus. We are not perfect, and we are always aware, like the apostle Paul, that the treasure of God's power and glory is at work within very human vessels (2 Corinthians 4:7). But as parents transparently follow Jesus "24/7," children have the greatest opportunity to see firsthand God's love and grace at work and can be inspired to follow Him as well.

To illustrate, when my husband or I encounter conflict with someone else in the community of faith, our daughters are very protective on our behalf. They watch closely to see how we will respond and are quick to defend us. In those real-life moments between Sundays in the privacy of our home, we can choose to exercise Christ's love and forgive or take offense and choose not to forgive. One is uniquely Christlike, liberating, and life-giving; the other is very human, emotionally and relationally crippling, and spiritually destructive. Our daughters can learn the Christian discipline of forgiveness by watching their parents practice a lifestyle of Jesus' forgiveness. We are saying by our actions, "Follow me (in forgiveness) as I follow Jesus (in forgiveness)." This is only one of many life-changing disciplines of faith in which children can be mentored at home to love and serve the Lord God with all of their hearts.

RECOGNIZE YOUR FAMILY AS A SMALL UNIT OF THE BODY OF CHRIST

During one of our times of ministry in India, I was requested to speak to faculty wives at Southern Asia Bible College. The question arose regarding how husbands should treat their wives. Given the very different ways in which husband-wife relationships are viewed in American and Indian cultures, I knew I would not serve them well by responding from my American cultural perspective. Suddenly the Holy Spirit dropped a truth into my heart as I looked into the faces of those sincere godly women.

The New Testament gives believers many instructions on

how to relate to fellow members of the Body of Christ. We are instructed to love one another (1 Peter 4:8; 1 John 3:11), encourage one another (1 Thessalonians 4:18; Hebrews 3:13), and be kind one to another (Ephesians 4:32). The apostle Paul's words to the Christians at Philippi are clear instructions in teaching fellow believers how to relate:

"Then make my joy complete by being like-minded, having the same love, being one in spirit and purpose. Do nothing out of selfish ambition or vain conceit, but in humility consider others better than yourselves. Each of you should look not only to your own interests, but also to the interests of others" (Philippians 2:2-4).

If husbands, wives, and their children are fellow believers, don't these relational instructions apply to family as well, regardless of our cultural background? Obeying and applying God's Word diligently inside as well as outside our homes assure us of God's blessings upon our obedience and in turn our families.

Some practical emotional, mental, and spiritual needs can be met uniquely within the Christian home when we are relating to one another not only as family but as fellow believers, as God's Word instructs. What are some ways that followers of Jesus can cultivate Christian community at home and simultaneously meet those needs?

1. Make home a place of physical, mental, emotional, and spiritual safety where family members are mutually committed to one another's well-being. A home of mental and spiritual safety is one in which it is safe for family members to ask sincere questions regarding God and His Word. No one asked more challenging questions regarding God and His purposes than the Psalmist David, and he was judged to be a man after God's own heart.

2. Recognize and respect the unique God-given gifts of each family member, encouraging and developing them for the fulfillment of God's purposes (1 Corinthians 12). As Paul's instructions teach us, each person's unique gifting is to be affirmed and valued for its potential in fulfilling God's purposes in the body of Christ and our world.

3. Integrate faith with the experiences of everyday life.
Discuss personal experiences of family members' days, being transparent about our human tensions and our desired response as Jesus' followers. Pray together about them honestly as they emerge. This encourages integrity and practicality in learning to love and serve God in a real and complex world.

4. Encourage family members to be globally aware and discuss the significance of world events from a biblical perspective. For example, why are tragic numbers of people in Africa dying of AIDS? What is our responsibility as Christians? What can we do as a family?

EMBRACE THE WORK OF THE HOLY SPIRIT WITHIN THE LIFE OF YOUR FAMILY

Pentecostal believers value the important work of the Holy Spirit within our lives as individuals and within our churches. However, are we guilty of underemphasizing and undervaluing the potential work of the Holy Spirit within our families in everyday life? How much more vital and compelling our faith can be if we engage life in the power of God's Spirit at home!

Look at the dynamic of the Holy Spirit in the Book of Acts immediately after the Day of Pentecost (Acts 3). His power was quickly demonstrated in and through the apostles and Early Church in the secular place as well as the sacred place. What might God do through His Spirit in our families if we were as expectant, open, and obedient to His leading and empowerment at home as we are in church? The Book of Acts is a dramatic first-century story of what happens when the Holy Spirit is at work. The following kinds of supernatural events still occur in the lives of 21st-century Spirit-filled believers as they participate in God's presence and power:

1. The Holy Spirit brings conviction of sin (John 16:7,8) and reveals Jesus as the Son of God (John 14:16,26). While we can teach our family members that we are all sinners in need of the saving, cleansing work of Jesus Christ, it is only the Holy Spirit who can convict of sin and reveal Jesus as one's Savior. It is the Holy Spirit who continues to convict us of actions and thoughts that are not like Jesus in our walk of faith.

2. The Holy Spirit sanctifies us, bringing freedom from sin for ongoing transformation into the likeness of Jesus Christ (Romans 8:2-4; 2 Corinthians 3:17,18). When even one family member is actively striving to follow Jesus more closely through the transforming work of the Holy Spirit, the whole family is affected. The potential for change is multiplied when several or all family members are united in seeking and yielding to the life-changing work of the Holy Spirit.

3. The Holy Spirit gives diverse spiritual gifts through which individual members of the community of faith are strengthened and encouraged (1 Corinthians 12–14). Gifts like words of wisdom and knowledge, faith, healing, and even miracles operating by the Spirit in our homes bring families closer to Jesus and one another as they serve God together.

Some of the most significant milestones in faith we experience as we follow Jesus can occur within the day-to-day life of our families. Moments of praying together for a sick child and experiencing the joy of God's healing, seeking guidance together for a parent's challenges at work and witnessing God's intervention, celebrating children's first attempts to share God's love with friends, learning to find strength in God and one another at the death of someone dear—all are steps in our family's journey of faith. And some days, I remember our daughter Jennifer's indignant question and have to smile.

Yes, God has called my husband to preach. *But does God make his schedule?*

Dr. Beth Grant is the wife of David Grant (Eurasia area director, Assemblies of God World Missions), and the mother of two daughters, Rebecca (25) and Jennifer (21). She is a missionary-educator for India and Eurasia (AGWM), and has spent 29 years in ministry throughout Eurasia. She serves as adjunct missions faculty at Evangel University and Assemblies of God Theological Seminary. Grant serves as chairperson for the National AG Task Force for Women in Ministry; co-founder and U.S. liaison for Project Rescue, a ministry to girl victims of sex trafficking; and serves on the Consortium of Faith-Based Initiatives Against Human Trafficking in Washington, D.C. Her earned degrees include an M.A. in cultural anthropology from AGTS in Springfield, Missouri, and a Ph.D. in intercultural education from the Biola UN School of Intercultural Studies in Los Angeles.

CHAPTER 18

The Epiphany

PETE VOSSLER

Let's get something straight from the outset; I am just a normal man. My wife, Janet, is just a normal woman. We are not wiser, stronger, bigger, faster, or more spiritual than anyone else. Why does this matter? The story you're about to read may seem unreal, but it happened just like I'm telling you.

One morning I woke up and found that I had placed my family in financial jeopardy. I will not take the time to reveal how. Suffice it to say, we were $75,000 in debt. All of this was on credit cards.

I was a preacher. God in His faithfulness was using me in spite of my failure to follow good, godly, sound financial practices. Even though I was struggling and trying to grasp how to handle this spiraling financial disaster, the Lord was still building the church we pastored in Sparks, Nevada. People were getting saved, healed, and baptized; but their leader had a big flaw.

I found myself asking God, "What, where, when, how? Help me, Lord!"

Through all of this we were faithful to tithe, believing that the Lord was our only hope. I believe in the tithe process now more than ever. But money management is more than being faithful in tithing. Most Christians believe the tithe principle is the main focus of the Bible when it comes to the subject of money. But there is so much more in God's Word about finance. In fact, I have found more about good, sound financial principles outlined in God's Word than about tithing. If a person only tithes, but does not follow a program of good financial stewardship, he or she will still go broke. Mathematics is a true science. Two plus two will always equal four. The greatest Christian in the world cannot violate the truths of financial math and expect the Lord to bail them out.

So on with the story.

I remember the time, the day, and the place like it was yesterday. I had just returned from my dad's house with a check in my hand. It was a loan for a down payment on a house. I was over 40 years old. I had a wife and two kids. I was still looking to Dad for a handout, and then it struck me like lightning—my first epiphany. *Your children might need to borrow money from you for a house and here you are still on the dole at 42 years of age. Grab hold of God and get it right.*

At that moment our life began to change.

Our children were 12 and 9 years old at the time. Like most parents, we justified many of our credit expenditures with our love for our children. We wanted to make sure that our kids could have what they needed and do what our society expected of them (and us). Janet and I made sure we had what we thought we needed also. What a trap! Sinking our teeth into the Madison Avenue cake was like shackling our life and future with chains. We had sold ourselves to the American way. Where could we go from here? How could we start over?

The key to success can be found in the Book. You know, God's Word. We were in trouble. We needed the Spirit. God's Word tells us the Holy Spirit will teach us all things (John 14:26). "Help us God," we pleaded. "We repent! Where do we begin?"

The Spirit led me to the Book of Ecclesiastes. I underlined every Scripture dealing with money and then read them in one sitting. They became my foundation. We know that wisdom, knowledge, and every perfect gift come from the Father (James 1:5,17).

The second step was to study every piece of "secular" knowledge on finance and investing and apply it in the light of God's Word. I read, devoured, discovered, and followed good financial advice from speakers, authors, and people I trusted and respected. When I became obedient to the full council of God, God came through.

The journey to financial health was not easy. In fact, at times it was downright hard. Moments of victory followed by areas of defeat became commonplace. Old habits are hard to break.

Justifying expenditures we could not afford was a big hurdle to overcome. Two Scriptures became our anchor during the journey. When we would fail, the Word would come in and lift us up. Galatians 6:9 states that we should "not become weary in doing good, for at the proper time we will reap a harvest if we do not give up" (NIV). Philippians 1:6 spoke volumes in times of need: "Being confident of this, that he who began a good work in you will carry it on to completion until the day of Christ Jesus."

How did the recovery happen? What was the process? We were pastoring a growing, thriving church. I was also driving a truck in the early mornings for the Post Office, and my wife was working full-time. We were faithful to tithe. We were faithful to pay down debt and we were faithful to follow and invest as the Lord outlined in Ecclesiastes 11:1-6. We funded my wife's 401K, my 403B, and learned other investment vehicles. As we listened and obeyed, God never ceased to deliver upon His promises.

On March 15, 2004, my second epiphany came, in of all places, Barnes and Noble. A staff member had given me a gift certificate to Barnes and Noble for Christmas and I purposely went to purchase a book on finance. I had been reading as many financial titles as I could put my hands on for the previous six years. I scrutinized the new books on the shelves: *The Richest Man in Babylon, Eight Steps to Seven Figures, Rich Dad Poor Dad*, just to name a few. I had read them all. It seemed every subject had been covered. There was nothing new I could read. The good fight was finished. The race had been run.

Janet and I had a moment of sudden intuitive understanding. We had a flash, an insight. The Lord was faithful. He had given us guidance and carried us upon His wings. We had become debt free. More than that, a miracle of another dimension had taken place. Our life had found new meaning.

In October of 1992, we had moved to Sparks, Nevada, to plant a church for the Northern California/Nevada District of the Assemblies of God. We had presented our fledgling congregation with a 10-year plan. For 10 years we had faithfully executed that plan. God had blessed us and we were now pastoring a wonderful, thriving church. We loved the church. The church loved us. But, we had completed the plan. Now what? Was this the end? Were we to move on? I could not get direction for our next 10 years at this ministry in Sparks.

The second epiphany was that we were totally financially free. Not only had the Lord led us out of the valley, He had placed us on a mountaintop. Some would shout hallelujah! But our hearts became burdened again as we searched for God's will for us and for the church He had led us to plant so many years earlier. We needed a new vision for life and ministry. And God delivered.

"If the Son sets you free, you will be free indeed" (John 8:36). This verse took on new meaning. We were free in finance and this brought on a freedom of spiritual vision. New life was breathed into ministry. We sensed a new focus and made new plans. The church began to grow again and, yes, we received a new 10-year vision.

Financial freedom has brought a deep, abiding peace and with it a gratitude to the Lord in a dimension that was not present before. Who are we that God should shower such great blessing on us? We are blessed to have His divine favor. A Scripture passage has become rich and real to us. It is our battle cry, for it has held us up when we have been tried and tested by fire and has brought us through as precious gold: "'Not by might nor by power, but by my Spirit,' says the Lord Almighty" (Zechariah 4:6).

Who are we? We are not rich, special, great, or extraordinary. We are children of the living God. If we are to be truly free indeed, then financial freedom must be part of the equation. Press in, look up, and follow Him. He will never disappoint.

Pete Vossler is senior pastor of Crosswinds Assembly of God in Sparks, Nevada. He and his wife, Janet, planted the church in their home in October of 1992 and have continued ministering as the church has grown into extensive ministry facilities. Crosswinds received the Church of the Year award from the Northern California/Nevada District of the Assemblies of God in 2001.

Vossler has been in the ministry for 20 years. He received a B.A. in music from Bethany University in Scotts Valley, California. He also attended San Jose State University and Lassen Junior College in Susanville, California.

Pete and Janet are very active in sports, love travel, and are active in business development. They have been married for 31 years. They have one son, Trei, 23, and one daughter, Karissa, 20.

CHAPTER 19

The Power of Verbal Blessing

AARON FRUH

The old adage "Sticks and stones may break my bones, but words will never harm me" is simply not true. God's Word tells us, "Pleasant words are like a honeycomb, sweetness to the soul and health to the bones" (Proverbs 16:24, NKJV). However, the opposite is also true. Destructive words bring bitterness to the soul and frailty to the bones.

Verbal blessing and affirmation are emotional building blocks that are vital in our walk with Christ. Listen to the following wisdom from the Book of Proverbs: "A man has joy by the answer of his mouth, and a word spoken in due season, how good it is!" (15:23). "A word fitly spoken is like apples of gold in settings of silver" (25:11). "Anxiety in the heart of man causes depression, but a good word makes it glad" (Proverbs 12:25).

Verbal abuse, on the other hand, is tragically destructive. Words like "You're fat," "You're stupid," "You're ugly," "You will never amount to anything," can stick to us like glue for a lifetime. Words can severely diminish a person's self-concept to the point where he or she is unable to establish long-lasting relationships with others. A person whose identity has been repeatedly attacked will learn to live either under the banner of extreme worthlessness or under the banner of artificial independence and self-sufficiency.

ARSENAL OF ABUSE

Consider these types of abuse. Each can have a verbal component.

- •Degrading—Minimizing the worth and value of another person through casting shame and ridicule.
- •Terrorizing—Threatening physical harm if expectations are not met; removing the safety of unconditional love and acceptance from a relationship.
- •Exploiting—Modeling and mentoring control, manipulation, and power over another for the abuser's own benefit.
- •Rejecting—Closing the door and pulling the shade of relationship in order to gain a temporary sense of power and control.
- •Corrupting—Accusing another of behaviors with low value to the point that the person begins to act them out.
- •Isolating—Separating a person from social interaction with others; gaining a sense of power through the confinement and boundaries placed on another.
- •Neglecting—Overlooking and minimizing the most basic of life needs. Verbally, this can be a complete lack of affirmation.

The tongue's power to destroy is virtually limitless. "And the tongue is a fire, a world of iniquity. The tongue is so set among our members that it defiles the whole body, and sets on fire the course of nature; and it is set on fire by hell. . . . But no man can tame the tongue. It is an unruly evil, full of deadly poison. With it we bless our God and Father, and with it we curse men, who have been made in the similitude of God. Out of the same mouth proceed blessing and cursing. My brethren, these things ought not to be so" (James 3:6,8-10).

A person who has consistently been degraded and terrorized by an abusive tongue filled with iniquity tends to lose all sense of stability and grounding. As iniquity is passed down, a new generation is stripped of its protective covering and is, in turn, bruised. This is what God was describing in Exodus 34:7. Left uncovered and rejected by the previous generation, a new generation loses its self-control.

HONESTY AND HEALING

The pathway toward healing our generational wounds starts by recognizing the things that have happened to us are not the last word on who we are. If we continually identify ourselves as victims of emotional and verbal abuse, we will keep a victim's mentality. True healing begins when we recognize unresolved generational issues we are carrying, when we see we are wearing someone else's emotional costume.

Healing transgenerational verbal abuse takes more than simply identifying and renouncing a bondage or iniquity that has been left for us to contend with. We must break the chains to the past by forgiving our abusers and becoming people of blessing.

Jesus commands us to bless the very ones who have injured us with destructive words: "Love your enemies, bless those who curse you, do good to those who hate you, and pray for those who spitefully use you and persecute you" (Matthew 5:44). Jesus himself was verbally despised and rejected even as He was physically abused. In fact, He took upon himself all of the curses of iniquity that you would endure. "He was wounded for our transgressions, He was bruised for our iniquities" (Isaiah 53:5).

We must come to the place in our walk with Christ that we understand that the abusive words spoken over us are not the last words on who we are. Our identity is found in the One who calls us by name! Take a look at the conversations Jesus had with people and you get a glimpse into His passion to verbally bless and affirm.

AFFIRMED BY THE MASTER

After Peter had confessed His faith in the lordship of Christ, Jesus answered him and said: "Blessed are you, Simon Bar-jonah, for flesh and blood has not revealed this to you, but My Father who is in heaven. And I also say to you that you are Peter, and on this rock I will build My church" (Matthew 16:17,18).

In the original language the verbal exchange here is thrilling. The name Peter comes from the Greek word *petros* and means "rock." Peter was anything but a rock. He was quick-tempered, impatient, and had a very volatile personality. He had become what his name Simon defined: a "reed" that blew in all directions when a light wind came up. Jesus knew that Peter was anything but a rock, but He blessed him and said: "Simon, I call you now what you shall later become—a rock of faith!"

Peter became known as one of the pillars in the church. History tells us that when the apostle Peter was martyred by crucifixion he requested to be hung upside down because he did not feel worthy to die in the same way as his Lord. Rock-like character indeed. A reed changed into a rock through the power of Christ's verbal blessing.

Once on His way from Judea to Galilee, Jesus went out of His way in order to minister to a Samaritan woman at Jacob's well. To do this Jesus had to break all cultural boundaries. First of all a Jewish man could never speak to a woman in public. Second, Jewish people hated Samaritans. Third, Jews would never touch the utensils or vessels of a Samaritan woman because the rabbis taught that Samaritan women were unclean from birth. So, when this Samaritan woman came to draw water the first words that Jesus spoke to her were stunning: "Give Me a drink" (John 4:7). For Jesus to drink from the woman's cup He would have had to touch it and this was unheard of.

Notice the woman's response: "How is it that You, being a

Jew, ask a drink from me, a Samaritan woman?" (John 4:9). With just four simple words of acceptance and affirmation Jesus pierced through her shame and opened the door to her heart. Later on, this woman's testimony of the short conversation she had with Jesus changed the entire city of Sychar: "And many of the Samaritans of that city believed in Him because of the word of the woman who testified, 'He told me all that I ever did'" (John 4:39). Think of it! A five-time divorcee with deep issues of rejection (many believe that this woman was barren and that is why her husbands divorced her) becomes an evangelist who shakes a city all because of Jesus' affirming words.

To His disciples Jesus said, "No longer do I call you servants, for a servant does not know what his master is doing; but I have called you friends, for all things that I heard from My Father I have made known to you" (John 15:15). Jesus approaches men and women everywhere who are filled with worthlessness, shame, and bitterness of soul, and speaks the words "no longer." No longer will you be called "Reed," now you will be called "Rock." No longer will you be called "slaves," now you will be called "friends." No longer will you be rejected, now you are accepted among the beloved.

FORGETTING AND GROWING

We can learn a wonderful lesson from the life of Joseph. His dreams, which spoke of his fruitful future, caused him to be hated and despised by his brothers. In fact, they did not have a kind word to say to him. Verbally assaulted, rejected, thrown into a pit of despair, and later sold into slavery and sent to prison, Joseph could have easily fallen prey to the verbal iniquity that plagued him.

We get a glimpse into the heart of this man of God when he named the two sons born to him in Egypt. He could have named them "Bitterness" and "Rejection." Instead Joseph named his firstborn "Manasseh," which means "Making

Forgetful." Joseph said that God had caused him to forget all the pain of growing up in an abusive home. The second son he named "Ephraim," which means "Fruitfulness." Joseph said that God had caused him to be fruitful, fulfilled, and whole in the land of great affliction.

Today every Friday evening in Jewish homes around the world, parents lay hands on their children and pronounce this blessing: "May God make you as Ephraim and as Manasseh!" In other words, "May you forget all the pain of your past and may you be fruitful in your future!"

When I first began to understand this wonderful truth I asked my 9-year-old daughter Hannah to sit down next to me so that I could speak a word of blessing over her life. Her response? "But Daddy, I didn't sneeze!" We reserve our blessings for the food and for those with allergies but Scripture calls us to go further. Parents consistently brought their children to Jesus that He might lay His hands upon them and verbally bless them.

The last act of Christ at His ascension was to stretch out His hands towards His disciples and verbally pronounce a blessing over them. "And He led them out as far as Bethany, and He lifted up His hands and blessed them. Now it came to pass, while He blessed them, that He was parted from them and carried up into heaven" (Luke 24:50,51). When we walk with Jesus and are daily affirmed by His written Word and by the comforting presence of the Holy Spirit we should in turn become instruments of blessing. The things God is doing on the inside of us should be expressed through our words of blessing toward others.

The words we speak do matter. Proverbs 18:21 says, "Death and life are in the power of the tongue, and those who love it will eat its fruit." You may have become emotionally barren because of death-bearing words spoken over you as a child, but you can stop the cycle of transgenerational verbal abuse. The coming generations after you can be like a fruitful, life-bearing tree as you imitate Jesus through a life of verbal blessing.

This little word "bless" comes from the Hebrew word *barak* and it simply means to "verbally confer benefit or affirmation." God said to Abraham in Genesis 22:17, "[In] blessing I will bless you." In other words, "In verbally affirming others, I will verbally affirm you!" This is a wonderful promise! Peter tells us that our inherited blessing depends on the verbal blessing that flows from our tongue, "not returning evil for evil or reviling for reviling, but on the contrary blessing, knowing that you were called to this, that you may inherit a blessing" (1 Peter 3:9).

A life of fruitfulness, wholeness, and resolution is ahead for all of those who will begin to verbally bless others. As you break the chains to your past hurts caused by verbal assault and as you begin a life of fruitfulness through a tongue filled with verbal blessing, the generations coming after you will never suffer from the destructive words you endured. May we who walk daily with Jesus be instruments of His blessing to others.

Aaron Fruh is the pastor of Knollwood Church in Mobile, Alabama. He is a graduate of Bethany University in Santa Cruz, California, and Wheaton Graduate School in Wheaton, Illinois. He is the author of two books published by Chosen Books: The Decree of Esther *and* The Forgotten Blessing. *Aaron and his wife, Sharon, have four children: Rachel, Elizabeth, Hannah and Nathan.*

CHAPTER 20

Four Character Traits in Sharing Jesus

MARK ELLIOTT

A recent article listed the five most popular New Year's resolutions. Taking up a new hobby, making more money, improving relationships, and giving up cigarettes were five through two on the list. Number one? Perhaps you guessed it—losing weight.

After the overindulgence of the holidays, we're quick to make resolutions to change our habits and our way of life. A new year gives us an opportunity to start fresh and better ourselves. But by the end of January we somehow forget our resolutions and go back to our old ways.

There is, however, one resolution every Christian should make and never forget—we are to be passionate in telling people about God's grace through His Son, Jesus Christ. Make no bones about it; we are to actively share the good news of Jesus Christ.

Jesus said in Matthew 28:19,20, "Therefore go and make disciples of all nations, baptizing them in the name of the Father and of the Son and of the Holy Spirit, and teaching them to obey everything I have commanded you" (NIV). That's our Great Commission. Pastor Rick Warren has said, "A great commitment to the Great Commandment and the Great Commission will build a great church."

In order to fulfill this mandate we need to develop convincing ways to persuade our friends, co-workers, and family members of their need for Jesus. When you enthusiastically tell people what you've discovered in Jesus Christ, they think it's too good to be true; they suspect there's a catch. There isn't. Jesus really does love them and has incredible things in store for their lives.

Let me share with you four character traits we can develop as Christians to share our faith successfully with those around us.

SINCERITY

If we are going to successfully share Christ with others, people must see in us a noticeable sincerity. James 3:17 says, "But the wisdom that comes from heaven is first of all pure; then peace-loving, considerate, submissive, full of mercy and good fruit, impartial and sincere."

People need to see more than anything else in us as Christians that we are sincere about our faith. Acts 2 tells about the Early Church and how it grew and won so many people to Christ. The process was pretty basic. "They broke bread in their homes and ate together with glad and sincere hearts" (Acts 2:46).

Sincerity is vital. Nothing turns people off to the gospel more than phony Christians. Yet we are so tempted to try to cover up, to be deceptive, to act religious, and to pretend we are holy. It is hard to admit to our imperfections. We are used to putting on masks that make others think we are better than we really are. But no one is perfect. We will attract the world's interest in our faith far more by simply being open about who we really are. You won't influence your friends who don't know Christ if you try to convince them that you never fall or stumble. They'll see right through you. Why not be honest in the first place?

If we are going to influence our community for Christ we need to be honest with ourselves and honest with the world and openly admit we are no better than anybody else. The church is full of imperfect people. In fact, all of us who are sincere will admit that if it were not for Jesus Christ our lives would be in turmoil.

PASSIONATE CONVICTION

Someone once said, "One man with conviction is worth more than 99 with mere opinions." Conviction is a strong belief that elicits a deep emotion.

In Acts 17:16 we read that the apostle Paul entered the city of Athens and while he was waiting for Timothy and Silas to join him, "he was greatly distressed to see that the city was full of idols." Athens was a city that had some 30,000 statues made in honor of 30,000 gods. Paul probably took a tour of Athens to see what the city was like, and as he walked around it distressed him to see all the pagan worship going on.

We also see the invasion of false religion happening around us. It disturbs me that pagan gods are trying to fill the spiritual void in people's lives, and yet these misinformed people are being led astray. It compels me even more to share Jesus with lost people.

If you don't passionately believe what you are saying, people will know. Your belief in Jesus has to be passionate in order to be contagious. It has to be something that comes from deep within your soul. Jesus Christ must be the greatest passion in your soul. His presence must exude from every pore of your being.

The prophet Jeremiah described the Word of God this way: "His word is in my heart like a fire, a fire shut up in my bones. I am weary of holding it in; indeed, I cannot" (Jeremiah 20:9). That is the kind of passionate conviction we need to motivate us to share Jesus Christ. Enthusiasm and passion often go a long way in convincing someone about Jesus.

SPIRITUAL RELIANCE

If we are going to share Jesus with people, we must not rely on human effort. We are God's servants, but it is the Holy Spirit who wins people to Jesus Christ. That is why each of us must value prayer if we desire to speak to our friends about our faith. Before we speak to people about Jesus we need the Holy Spirit to work on their hearts. Jesus said in John 15:26 that it is the Holy Spirit who testifies to the world about Him.

God wants us to pray that the kingdom of heaven will expand on earth. In John 14:14 Jesus said, "You may ask me for anything in my name, and I will do it." If we ask for souls, we will receive them. James wrote, "You do not have, because you do not ask God" (James 4:2).

When you pray for the lost, consider these questions:

• Are you praying for the lost people you know to be healed and set free from Satan's bondage? (Acts 3:16; 10:34-38; James 5:13-16; 1 John 5:16,17)

• Are you praying for them to be saved? (James 5:20; 1 John 5:16,17)

• Are you praying with the conviction that only Jesus can change people and it is our duty to pray for them and to be a positive Christian influence? (John 3:21; 6:44-47; 13:8; 1 Corinthians 3:5-9; Hebrews 5:2; 1 John 3:16-20; 4:12)

Often the most effective thing you can do to see a person come to faith in Christ is to pray for him or her. Don't speak a word to them until you have first prayed for them deeply and passionately. Can I ask you to choose a few local people in your life who you know need Jesus and pray for them for the next few weeks or months? After you have prepared their heart with prayer, then speak with them about your own personal faith in Christ.

Martin Luther said, "As is the business of tailors to make clothes and of cobblers to mend shoes, so it is the business of Christians to pray."

APPEALING URGENCY

Often we are too passive about sharing our faith. On the one hand, there is clearly a level of aggressiveness that repels people. But I believe most Christians go too far in the other direction and have such a casual, nonchalant spirit about sharing Christ that people don't even know they are Christians. A recent church study revealed that 95 percent of evangelical Christians admitted they had never led anyone to the Lord. We are too passive about reaching lost people.

Paul said, "We implore you on Christ's behalf: Be reconciled to God" (2 Corinthians 5:20). Paul implored; he never casually invited. A few verses later, he said, "Now is the time of God's favor, now is the day of salvation" (6:2). For Paul, there was no time other than now to accept Christ. Never leave the impression that it doesn't matter whether or not someone comes to faith in Christ. Time is running short and today is the best day for salvation. We need to be urgent about people who are lost. "How, then, can they call on the one they have not believed in? And how can they believe in the one of whom they have not heard? And how can they hear without someone preaching to them?" (Romans 10:14).

John Harper was born into a Christian family on May 29, 1872, in Glasgow, Scotland. In 1912, Harper, the newly called pastor of Moody Church in Chicago, was traveling on the *Titanic* with his 6-year-old daughter, Nana. After the ship struck an iceberg and began to sink, he got Nana into a lifeboat but apparently made no effort to follow her. Instead, he ran through the ship yelling, "Women, children, and unsaved into the lifeboats!" Survivors reported that he then began witnessing to anyone who would listen. He continued preaching even after he had jumped into the water and was clinging to a piece of wreckage. (He'd already given his lifejacket to another man.)

A survivor of the *Titanic* recounted Harper's final moments four years later at a meeting in Hamilton, Ontario. "When I was drifting alone that awful night," the man said, "the tide brought Pastor Harper near me on a piece of wreckage. 'Man,' he said, 'are you saved?' 'No,' I said. He replied, 'Believe on the Lord Jesus Christ and you will be saved.'

"The waves bore him away, but, strange to say, brought him back a little later, and he said, 'Are you saved now?' 'No,' I said, 'I cannot honestly say that I am.' He said again, 'Believe on the Lord Jesus Christ, and you will be saved.' Shortly after, he went down. There, alone in the night, and with two miles of water under me, I believed! I am John Harper's last convert."

He was also one of only six people picked out of the water by the lifeboats; the other 1,522, including Harper, died in the cold.

Friends, let's make it our life's mission to be as urgent about lost souls as John Harper was. May even our last moments be used to win the lost to Christ. The renowned colonial preacher George Whitefield once said, "O Lord give me souls, or take my soul!" We will only see our churches grow as we take seriously God's call to us to share the good news with those who are lost and going to hell. May this be a year of multiplication in your life and the life of your home church as you resolve to share Jesus!

Remember, "A great commitment to the Great Commandment and the Great Commission builds a great church!" Take time today to pray for your lost friends. Then invite them to attend church with you this Sunday.

Dr. W. Mark Elliott was born and raised in the rolling hills of southern Indiana. He entered the full-time pastoral ministry in 1982. He holds two master's degrees and completed a doctor of ministry degree in 2005. He is currently the lead pastor of New Life Community Church in Oshkosh, Wisconsin. He has served at churches as small as 20 as a church planter and as large as 4,900 as the small group pastor in Naperville, Illinois. Pastor Elliott has been happily married for 25 years and is the father of four children, ages 8, 12, 16, and 19. He enjoys travel, golf, sports, and reading.

Section

5

"When met with faith, tests equip us to carry out God's purposes."

—Brad Trask

CHAPTER 21

Grade-A Faith

BRAD TRASK

Remember that sinking feeling you had in school when your teacher suddenly asked your class to take out your pencils and clear your desks to take a test? You thought you knew the material, but the sudden need to apply it caught you off guard.

In some ways, faith operates that way in our lives. We study the Word. We exercise our faith daily in prayer and worship. We feel like we know what faith is and how it should operate in our lives. But then the unexpected catches us at a low moment. We're caught off guard. Our faith begins to falter.

Receiving an A in "Faith 101" is imperative to the follower of Christ. The apostle James states, "Consider it pure joy, my brothers, whenever you face trials of many kinds, because you know that the testing of your faith develops perseverance. Perseverance must finish its work so that you may be mature and complete, not lacking anything. . . . Blessed is the man who perseveres under trial, because when he has stood the test, he will receive the crown of life that God has promised to those who love him" (James 1:2-4,12, NIV).

"Trials" is a translation of the Greek word *peirasmos,* which can also be translated "testings." While we may reach an age where academic classrooms and tests cease, our spiritual classroom experience never ends. Throughout our lives our Heavenly Father at times says, "Take out your pencils and clear your desks." But He always does so with the view of developing perseverance in our walk of faith. He already sees the crown of life He has in store for us.

Let's evaluate the importance of becoming a lifelong learner in our faith in preparation for those times of testing. I'd like to suggest to you four criteria for life's testing times that will give you a solid understanding of where your faith is today and where God can take it.

THE INEVITABILITY OF TESTS

The apostle James writes, "Consider it pure joy . . . *whenever* you face trials." Not *if*, but *whenever* you face trials. Jesus did not escape trials while on this earth; neither will we. King David said, "Many are the afflictions of the righteous, but the Lord delivers him out of them all" (Psalm 34:19, NKJV).

In life, as in the classroom, there are three types of people. There are those taking a test, those who have just finished taking a test and those who are preparing for a test. The Bible says, "Man is born to trouble as surely as sparks fly upward" (Job 5:7, NIV). God did not save us to exempt us from tests; rather, He sent His Son to help us with the tests. Be cautious concerning doctrine that promotes, "Once you become a Christian it's all about the honey and not the bees." The fact of the matter is, the stronger a Christian one becomes, the more severe the tests will become. Paul the apostle said, "Everyone who wants to live a godly life in Christ Jesus will be persecuted" (2 Timothy 3:12). Notice those words "everyone" and "will be."

Biblical examples abound regarding this topic. Job was a blameless man who feared God and shunned evil. However, in a single day Job lost his family, finances, fortune, fitness, and friends. Joseph, a man of unquestioned integrity within Potiphar's home, was thrown into prison for a crime he didn't commit. Daniel was totally committed to God in the face of adversity, and he found himself in a den of lions.

None of us should think it strange to experience difficulty

while serving the Lord. Peter said, "Do not be surprised at the painful trial you are suffering, as though something strange were happening to you" (1 Peter 4:12). Jesus himself said, "In this world you will have trouble" (John 16:33). Tests are a certainty in life.

THE DIVERSITY OF TESTS

James says, "Consider it pure joy . . . whenever you face trials of *many* kinds." This reminds us that life is touched by a variety of tests. Tests can be physical, financial, psychological, spiritual, or emotional, with subtle combinations as well. They can also vary in their difficulty. There are the mild irritations that complicate an hour or a day. There are monumental tragedies that alter the very landscape of life.

Tests come in as wide a variety as the people who encounter them. And in God's economy, that translates into a wonderful resource for the believer. Within the body of Christ, there are always going to be brothers and sisters who have faced circumstances similar to our own. As Paul wrote to the Corinthians, "We can comfort those in any trouble with the comfort we ourselves have received from God" (2 Corinthians 1:4).

THE PURPOSEFULNESS OF TESTS

We may never comprehend many specifics about the tests of life. However, if as followers of Christ we comprehend "that the testing of your faith develops perseverance," we will succeed.

When looking at the word for "test" in this passage of Scripture, picture a young bird that is testing its wings. The point of this image is to reinforce the concept that something (wings) is ready to perform the function for which it was created. The word "test" refers also to the refining of gold. As gold is subjected to extreme temperatures the purification process burns off the impurities. It is important for us to understand that life's tests are for our refinement.

When met with faith, tests equip us to carry out God's purposes. The opposite is also true. If we fail to apply our faith during testing times, we're left with our own miserable strength. Solomon said, "If you falter in times of trouble, how small is your strength!" (Proverbs 24:10).

One may not know the *when* of tests; they can happen any time. One may not know the *why* of tests; they can seemingly have no rhyme or reason. One may not know the *where* of tests; they can happen any place. Elisabeth Elliot said, "Every experience of trial puts us to this test: Do we trust God or don't we?"

THE DEPENDABILITY OF TESTS

Tests are built into the design of most classrooms because they have been proven dependable in creating solid learning among students. God's design allows for tests in our spiritual experience as well. When we recognize God at work through our tests, we learn to rejoice in them. We learn to celebrate that God is placing within our lives the potential to receive an A in the area of faith.

At the core of each test God is really asking us two questions: "Will you trust Me?" and "How much do you trust Me?" Our joy in the midst of our tests comes when we recognize God's tests are dependable; they are designed to strengthen our lives, preparing us for the most effective service in the Kingdom. Three elements comprise this fourth category of rejoicing and dependability.

God is always revealed. God permits trouble to come into our lives so that we will draw close to Him. Our human tendency is to stray from God when life is in a nontesting mode. Tests have a unique propensity to draw us back to God. C.S. Lewis wrote, "God whispers to us in our pleasures but He shouts to us in our pain. Suffering is God's megaphone to rouse a deaf world." Lewis made this statement after caring for his wife, who died of cancer.

The three Hebrews who were thrown into a Babylonian fiery furnace experienced this same revelation (Daniel 3). While only three men were thrown into the furnace, a fourth showed up, the Son of God. In the midst of an inferno meant to destroy, divine revelation occurred—in the person of Jesus Christ. Often God permits the furnaces of life so that He may reveal himself to us in unique ways. Charles Spurgeon stated, "The refiner is never far from the furnace when his gold is in the fire." The Bible declares, "When you pass through the waters, I will be with you; and when you pass through the rivers, they will not sweep over you. When you walk through the fire, you will not be burned; the flames will not set you ablaze . . . for I am with you" (Isaiah 43:2,5).

We are always refined. Your faith may have impurities; therefore, God allows tests to remove the dross. A suffering crippled woman came to her pastor, weeping and shaken in her faith. She asked, "Why has God made me like this?" He prudently replied, "God has not made you—He is making you!"

Remember, God may not ignite the fire of affliction, but He does control the thermostat. The Psalmist said, "It was good for me to be afflicted so I might learn your decrees" (119:71). There are certain lessons in life that are only learned during times of testing. When pleading with the Lord to turn down the heat, evaluate if you are responding correctly to the refining process. Just as a silversmith looks into a crucible and watches as the impurities float to the top, so God watches to see our sinful tendencies separate from the molten silver of our lives.

An anonymous poet said it like this:

When God wants to drill a man,
And thrill a man, and skill a man,
When God wants to mold a man,
To play the noblest part;

When He yearns with all His heart,
To create so great and bold a man
That all the world shall be amazed;
Watch His methods, watch His ways!

How He ruthlessly perfects
Whom He royally elects!
How He hammers him and hurts him,
And with mighty blows converts him

Into trial shapes of clay which
Only God understands;
While his tortured heart is crying
And he lifts beseeching hands!

How He bends but never breaks
When his good He undertakes;
How He uses whom He chooses
And with every purpose fuses him;
By every act induces him
To try His splendor out—
God knows what He's about!

We are always rewarded. The apostle James stresses that there is a special crown waiting for the person who "has stood the test" (1:12). "Weeping may remain for a night, but rejoicing comes in the morning" (Psalm 30:5).

Yes, this life is difficult. Yes, our faith is tested. But no matter how difficult or prolonged the test, our reward will be eternal. Paul assures us, "Our light and momentary troubles are achieving for us an eternal glory that far outweighs them all" (2 Corinthians 4:17).

Martin Luther struggled through some severe tests. One day, his wife, Katie, came into his study wearing all black, her face covered by a veil.

"Who died?" Martin asked.

She solemnly responded, "God died."

Martin retorted, "Silly woman, God hasn't died."

"Oh," she replied, "I thought by the way you were acting that God had died."

The impact was immediate and reminded Luther that regardless of the tests he was facing, God was in control.

Is your faith being tested? Remind yourself that God is in control—and that you never have a testimony without a test. Then, get out your pencil and clear your desk. The next test is guaranteed.

Dr. Bradley T. Trask is senior pastor of Brighton Assembly of God in Brighton, Michigan. Trask and his wife, Rhonda, pioneered the work, which began in 1992. Over the past 14 years God has blessed his ministry, exemplified by the church's growing attendance and numerous ministries that have been implemented. Additionally, under Pastor Trask and Rhonda's leadership, the congregation of Brighton Assembly has developed a sincere desire to impact the world around them evidenced by their outward focus toward domestic and foreign missions giving and projects.

Trask was recently reelected as a sectional presbyter in the Michigan District and serves on the board of directors for Convoy of Hope, an international relief/compassion ministry. He serves on the Commission on Doctrinal Purity and the Ministerial Enrichment Committee for the Assemblies of God national office.

Trask is an ordained minister who holds a doctor of ministry degree from the Assemblies of God Theological Seminary. He also holds a master of divinity degree from AGTS and a bachelor of science degree from North Central University.

CHAPTER 22

Dealing With Difficult People: Seven Guiding Principles

JOHN C. MARTIN

Difficult people. Those two words tend to evoke an emotional response in us. The more we ponder the concept, the more likely images and faces come across the landscape of our mind. Whether it is the difficult person in the workplace or the family member who rubs you the wrong way, the fact is very simple. Every single one of us deals with difficult people.

Yet, we must remember that God loves the difficult person as much as He loves each of us. He sent His Son to die for that person as much as He sent His Son to die for us. God cares about that individual's situation in life as much as He cares about our circumstances. Our relationship with Jesus Christ means we must treat these situations as He would. So, as we think about how to best handle the difficult people in our lives, let me share with you seven guiding principles from Scripture.

WE ARE CALLED TO LIVE AT PEACE WITH ALL PEOPLE

Hebrews 12 states very clearly that we must "make every effort to live in peace with all men" (Hebrews 12:14, NIV). The call to peace is not an option. Rather, it is a mandate. In fact, the Lord wants us to work at this so intently that He says we should "make every effort." Don't just give it a good shot; give it your best shot! Peace does not come easily. It comes when people make it a priority.

Proverbs 19:11 states, "A man's wisdom gives him patience; it is to his glory to overlook an offense." Everyone has committed sin. We all have said things and done things in life we wish we had not. As humans, we make mistakes. If we are going to live at peace with one another, we must allow the guiding principle of overlooking the mistakes of others to take precedence.

WE MUST TAKE THE HIGH ROAD

The Bible says, "Do not repay evil with evil or insult with insult, but with blessing" (1 Peter 3:9). When someone treats us unkindly or poorly, we have a choice. Are we going to lash out at them? Are we going to treat them the same way they have treated us? Or are we going to take the high road in life and choose to not repay them for the things they have done to us?

When Jesus stood trial, He responded to the questions He was asked, but He was a Man of few words because He knew that defending His cause was going to be futile. He had already decided to follow the will of the Father, and He knew that it would eventually lead to His death. Lashing out in response to His accusers' threats or trying to convince the rulers and mob otherwise would get Him nowhere.

Jesus had a higher perspective. He knew that God the Father could "rescue" Him at any time, and it was only because God was allowing this to happen that it was actually taking place (John 19:11). So Jesus was obedient to the Father's will. He endured the incredible pain of being beaten and dying upon a cross knowing that this intense time would pass and victory for a greater cause would be won.

Taking the high road is about seeing things from God's perspective. Though the immediate pain of being mistreated can seem overwhelming, paying people back "evil with evil or insult with insult" is never the answer. Do not stoop to that level. Rather, take a lesson from Jesus, and choose to be silent instead of saying something both inappropriate and something you will later regret.

WE MUST OFFER FORGIVENESS FREELY

Forgiveness is not a feeling. If it were a feeling, most of us would never offer forgiveness because we would not feel like it. We would rationalize the feeling away and convince ourselves that the other person does not deserve the forgiveness.

Forgiveness is not forgetting. There is a huge difference between God and mankind. When God offers forgiveness, He says that He remembers our sins no more (Hebrews 8:12). As far as the east is from the west, God has removed our transgressions from us (Psalm 103:12). What an amazing concept! The God who spoke the world into existence chooses to remember our sins no more. Conversely, we do not have the ability to click off the memory button of our brain when we forgive someone. When we forgive, we remember. The difference is, when we forgive someone else, we allow God to heal the hurts and pains of the past.

Forgiveness is not excusing either. Just because we forgive somebody doesn't mean we are excusing someone for what has taken place. It means we are offering others grace in the midst of the mistakes they have made. Some people struggle in offering forgiveness because they believe they are condoning the inappropriate behavior of others. They feel that others should be held accountable for their actions. But forgiveness is not an option. "For if you forgive men when they sin against you, your heavenly Father will also forgive you. But if you do not forgive men their sins, your Father will not forgive your sins" (Matthew 6:14,15).

Forgiveness should be offered, even before it is requested. As Christians, we should be modeling this for the world around us. We should readily offer forgiveness to other people regardless of their desire to seek forgiveness from us. Occasionally, I hear some Christians saying that they are not going to offer forgiveness until the other party asks for it. I do not find that anywhere in Scripture. Forgiveness should always be offered, because it is the right thing to do. "Bear with each other and forgive whatever grievances you may have against one another. Forgive as the Lord forgave you" (Colossians 3:13).

WE MUST IDENTIFY WITH THE OTHER PERSON'S SITUATION

If we are going to have wisdom in dealing with difficult people, we must try to understand life from their point of view. The adage "seek first to understand, then to be understood" applies here.[1] In some instances, we may approach life differently from someone else. The fact remains, the more I can identify with and understand another person, the greater the opportunity of really getting along with them. Philippians 2:4 serves as a great reminder: "Each of you should look not only to your own interests, but also to the interests of others."

Recently, as a pastor, I became aware of a family's intense struggle. Multiple crises seemed to hit in a very short period of time. The Lord gave me great compassion for them. After I understood more of what they were dealing with, God changed my heart and helped me become more patient with them. Seek to understand the other person. It may change your whole perspective of the situation and your relationship with them.

WE MUST PRAY FOR THOSE WHO HURT US

There are a few verses in the Bible I do not particularly like. But God did not ask for my opinion; neither did He ask for yours. Our responsibility is to apply His Word to our lives and choose to be obedient to it. Matthew 5:44 says, "But I tell you: Love your enemies and pray for those who persecute you."

When we pray for those who have hurt us, we open up the door for God to place a love in our hearts for those who have wounded us. Though we may tend to think of prayer as communication with God in order to change other people and situations in life, I have found quite frequently that prayer is more about God changing me. God wants to direct our hearts, our attitudes, and our perspectives. When we pray, we open up a communication line with God that He uses to mold us into the people that He wants us to become.

At this critical juncture, either the breakthrough takes place or the enemy tends to get a foothold. When I pray for people who have hurt me, I must continue to pray for them until the Lord changes my attitude toward them. I must continue to pray for them, at the very least, until I have a love in my heart for them. If I give up praying without that breakthrough, I am allowing the enemy a dangerous opportunity to wreak havoc with my feelings and emotions. Over time, if left unchecked and unconfessed, the initial feelings of hurt, disappointment, frustration, and pain eventually turn into deep-seated jealousy, anger, bitterness, or depression.

WE MUST SPEAK THE TRUTH IN LOVE

I placed this principle toward the end of the list because there are a number of prerequisite guiding principles that must be demonstrated before we ever jump into this one. Having said this, there are moments when we need to speak out. There are times when an injustice has taken place and something needs to be said. There are occasions when people get way out of line and someone needs to stand up.

There are two important concepts related to this that must be kept in mind. First, if a difficulty can be worked out just between you and the person who has wronged you, do so. If not, resolve the conflict with a couple of witnesses (see Matthew 18:15). Keep the number of people involved in the conflict to a minimum. The more people that get involved, the more likely sides will be taken and the conflict will escalate. Second, let the love of Christ permeate your thinking and communication with others. If love and compassion are not at the foundation of the interaction, then the potential for a misunderstanding greatly increases.

Let me offer an additional word of caution. Sometimes we get ahead of God, and we choose to take matters into our own hands. Do not take on God's role. Let God be God. Instead of playing the Holy Spirit in someone else's life, sometimes we need to take a step back and allow the Lord to speak into others' lives in His timing. When God is not leading us and the timing is wrong, we can create more problems than we solve.

WE MUST ENTRUST EVERYTHING TO GOD

My two favorite verses in all of Scripture state: "Trust in the Lord with all your heart and lean not on your own understanding; in all of your ways acknowledge him, and he will make your paths straight" (Proverbs 3:5,6). Entrusting difficult people to God may not be easy, but it is best! Leaving the stresses and burdens of life with the Almighty One is the only wise choice. As we seek God's help and we entrust these situations to Him, the Lord will lead and direct us in the way we should go.

Dr. John C. Martin is senior pastor of Calvary Christian Assembly in Seattle, Washington. He has also pastored in Coulee City and served as executive director of the Division of *Church Ministries for the Northwest District Council of the Assemblies of God.*

Dr. Martin earned his B.A. at Northwest University in Kirkland, Washington, his master's in religious education at the Assemblies of God Theological Seminary in Springfield, Missouri, and his doctor of ministry at Fuller Theological Seminary in Pasadena, California. He remains actively involved at Northwest as an adjunct professor and member of the Pastors Advisory Board and School of Nursing Advisory Board.

Martin was selected citizen of the year in Coulee City in 1996.

John and Ronda Martin have two children, Rachel (13) and Joshua (10).

CHAPTER 23

The Challenge of Forgiveness

ERIC A. HANSEN

Even now, it's painful to think about. They hurt you real bad. When you weren't looking, Bam! They blindsided you, spoke evil about you, slipped a dagger between your fourth and fifth ribs; they told a lie about you and then acted as if nothing was wrong. Even now, it's painful to think about. You wake up in the morning with it on your mind. Sometimes you lie in bed at night thinking about it. It's constantly on your mind. You know you're thinking about it a lot more than you should but it consumes your thoughts.

Whether they hurt you on accident or on purpose, wouldn't it be nice if *at least* they said, "I'm sorry"? That's not asking too much, is it? I mean, it's the least they could do after all the trouble, heartache and pain they've caused.

Who was it that hurt you so badly? Was it a close friend? That was my case; he was a close associate. For you, perhaps it was a family member or business companion. For the purpose of making my point, I'd like for you to take that hurt you sense and set it aside for at least the next three minutes while you finish reading what I have to say. If you want to keep your anger, then you'll not want to read any further. However, know this if you choose to keep your anger: Unforgiveness is an acid that eats its own container.

HYPOCRITE!

Forgiveness is one of the great sails of our Gospel Ship. Without it we'll never enter heaven's port. C. S. Lewis said, "Everyone says forgiveness is a lovely idea, until they have something to forgive." Jesus said, "Why do you look at the speck of sawdust in your brother's eye and pay no attention to the plank in your own eye? How can you say to your brother, 'Let me take the speck out of your eye,' when all the time there is a plank in your own eye? You hypocrite, first take the plank out of your own eye, and then you will see clearly to remove the speck from your brother's eye" (Matthew 7:3-5, NIV).

What all that really means is that perhaps before you get all wrapped up in *your* pain and *your* hurts and how *you* feel and all *your* aches and injuries, perhaps you may want to consider what happened to Jesus. "He was oppressed, and he was afflicted, yet he opened not his mouth: he is brought as a lamb to the slaughter, and as a sheep before her shearers is dumb, so he openeth not his mouth" (Isaiah 53:7, KJV). What? Jesus was beaten, spat upon, cursed, whipped, and ridiculed, yet He didn't retaliate? Yes, it's true. There was no retaliation in Him. You may not want to hear that but, nonetheless, it's the truth. And He is to be our example. Jesus not only kept His mouth shut but went a step further and said, "Father, forgive them" (Luke 23:34).

GOD HAS SHOWN YOU WHAT TO DO

As a pastor, I've been wounded so badly (even by other Christians) that if I wasn't saved, I think I might actually have hurt someone. I'm serious. I'm being real and transparent. Forgiving has not always been easy for me, and even today at times I would rather pay my tithe four times over than have to forgive someone for hurting me or my family. But it doesn't work that way. The Lord requires mercy not judgment. "He has showed you, O man, what is good. And what does the

Lord require of you? To act justly and to love mercy and to walk humbly with your God" (Micah 6:8, NIV).

By now you may be saying, "All right, I give in! I'll forgive them. However, I'm going to keep a list and on that list next to their name is a little black mark that reminds me of their offense." Might I poke you yet one more time and remind you of Love's nature? "It is not rude, it is not self-seeking, it is not easily angered, it keeps *no* record of wrongs" (1 Corinthians 13:5, emphasis added).

HEAVEN'S LAW

If God has assembled His teachings in such a manner that forgiveness cannot be denied, it is ineffectual to persist in holding on to hatred and resentment. So I guess the real question should be, why fight it? Why not forgive them? Aren't you tired of having that old wound consume so much of your mental and emotional energy?

Whether they hurt you by accident or on purpose, it doesn't matter. You must come to terms with the fact that you may never hear those words "I'm sorry." And to let some other person, Christian or otherwise, keep you from standing in the flow of the Holy Spirit's love and power is absurd. I have decided that, regardless how egregious the offense against me, I will not let any other person come between me and my Heavenly Father's love and forgiveness. I must forgive.

A long time ago, Jesus spoke these words to His disciples when He was teaching them how to pray: "Forgive us our debts, as we also have forgiven our debtors" (Matthew 6:12). To me that really is the bottom line. If I want God to forgive me, I must, I'm obligated, I'm required, to forgive others. It's heaven's law.

Jesus lived by that law. He is our hero. He has modeled for us how we should react when we're wrongly accused and our character assaulted. He showed us that (in the words of Mark Twain) "forgiveness is the fragrance that the violet sheds on the heel that has crushed it." And God's fragrance is eternal life for anyone who would embrace the crushing of the cross.

"If you have any encouragement from being united with Christ, if any comfort from his love, if any fellowship with the Spirit, if any tenderness and compassion, then make my joy complete by being like-minded, having the same love, being one in spirit and purpose. Do nothing out of selfish ambition or vain conceit, but in humility consider others better than yourselves. Each of you should look not only to your own interests, but also to the interests of others. Your attitude should be the same as that of Christ Jesus" (Philippians 2:1-5).

If putting others first is a fundamental principle of your life, you will find it easier to forgive. When you put aside your own ambitions and conquer your foolish pride, you will focus on forgiveness instead of your own rights and privileges. When you determine that, with the Holy Spirit's help, your attitudes will mirror those of Jesus, His commitment to forgive a lost world becomes the model for your commitment to forgive those who have wronged you.

SEVEN HINTS TO WHOLENESS

1. Start by reminding yourself that compared to Christ's suffering you haven't been seriously wronged at all.

2. Pray that God will bless the one who has hurt you.

3. Personally look for a way to bless them.

4. If the sin against you is particularly hard to forget, try to ease the memory by thinking godly thoughts about those who have wronged you instead of hateful ones.

5. List the blessings of the Lord in your life.

6. Thank God for blessing you with His forgiveness.

7. Every night for a month, repeat slowly and thoughtfully that phrase from the Lord's Prayer, "Forgive me my sins, as I forgive those who have sinned against me."

DING, DONG, DING. . .

Corrie Ten Boom (a Holocaust survivor) told of not being able to forget a wrong that had been done to her. She had forgiven the person, but she kept rehashing the incident and so she couldn't sleep. Finally Corrie cried out to God for help in putting the problem to rest.

"God's help came in the form of a kindly Lutheran pastor," Corrie wrote in her journal, "to whom I confessed my failure after two sleepless weeks."

"Up in the church tower," the pastor said, nodding out the window, "is a bell which is rung by pulling on a rope. But you know what? After the sexton lets go of the rope, the bell keeps on swinging. First ding, then dong. Slower and slower until there's a final dong and it stops. I believe the same thing is true of forgiveness. When we forgive, we take our hand off the rope. But if we've been tugging at our grievances for a long time, we mustn't be surprised if the old angry thoughts keep coming for a while. They're just the ding-dongs of the old bell slowing down."

"And so it proved to be. There were a few more midnight reverberations, a couple of dings when the subject came up in my conversations, but the force—which was my willingness in the matter—had gone out of them. They came less and less often and at the last stopped altogether: we can trust God not only above our emotions, but also above our thoughts."[1]

Eric A. Hansen has been the lead pastor of iWorshipCenter.org in Springfield, Illinois, for 10 years. He is a graduate of North Central University of the Assemblies of God (B.A.) and Evangel Christian University (Th.M.). During Hansen's pastorate, the 100-member church has outgrown their facility, purchased 30 acres of land and is currently building a new facility to seat 850 people (Phase I). Hansen is a sought-after speaker. He oversees five additional churches that he has planted and hosts one national and three local television programs along with two radio programs. Hansen also sits on city and county governmental boards. Eric and his wife, Cheryl (who is also a credentialed minister and an RN), have one daughter, Hannah Jean, who has a desire to be a missionary in Asia.

CHAPTER 24

From Disappointment to Glory

CHARLES A. DAVIS

We are told that disappointments develop character and that character is seen in how we handle these setbacks of life. But how do we deal with our disappointments? Do we outwardly put on a good front and keep pressing forward while on the inside we are more doubtful and less trusting of God? Do we become bitter toward God because of our unmet expectations? Do we entertain thoughts of giving up?

The key to dealing with disappointments is to choose the right attitude. We must decide to live with the conviction that every time we are disappointed, God has something much better for us. As Jesus neared the end of His ministry on earth, His message took on a new dimension and urgency. The disciples had dreams of the Kingdom and the glory they would share, but Jesus spoke of suffering and death. The disciples' dreams and plans seemed finished, but Jesus was pointing them to something far greater than their dreams and plans.

THE GREAT QUESTION

"Who do the crowds say I am?" Jesus asked His disciples after He had fed a multitude (Luke 9:18, NIV). It is always easy to discuss "others" and "somebody else." There is no call for commitment and no pressure. It is not a personal question; it is an opinion poll. The disciples admitted that people were confused about Jesus' identity and some thought He might be a reincarnated prophet.

Jesus then asked this searching question: "But what about you? Who do you say I am?" (Luke 9:20). This, of course, is the greatest question of all. It is not *a* question; it is *the* question. It calls for a very personal and subjective response. Who is Jesus to me? No one can answer this question for us; we must discover this all-important truth for ourselves. Jesus called himself "Son of Man" more often than His rightful title "Son of God." He wanted to lead people to draw their own conclusion about Him. He allowed people to receive Him and He allowed them to reject Him. What is our answer to this question? Who is Jesus to us, and how does our answer to this question direct and affect all areas of our lives?

THE GREAT CONFESSION

Peter spoke. He usually did; shyness was never his gift. His quick response may indicate that this was a consensus decision of the entire group made at an earlier time. The disciples would have discussed this at length on many occasions. They knew exactly who Jesus was. That is why they were still with Him while others had defected. It was also a response based on divine revelation; God had given Peter this answer. Jesus had never asked this question of them in this way before, but since He asked, Peter did not hesitate.

When Peter declared what we now call his Great Confession, the dynamics of everything changed in an instant. What had been discussed in quiet was now out in the open. "You are the Christ, the Son of the living God" (Matthew 16:16). There—it is said. No one needs to whisper anymore. Jesus is the Messiah, the Promised Deliverer, the Anointed One. And the Son of Man in the presence of His disciples fully accepted the title Son of God.

We can only imagine all of the expectations that now surfaced for Peter and the others. If Jesus allowed His followers to finally declare in the open that He is the Christ, then the Kingdom Age has come! From the time of Abraham, the people of God had been waiting, longing, and praying for the Christ. If Jesus will admit He is the Messiah, heaven has come to earth. All that the prophets wrote about would now come to pass. And, certainly, all of the disciples' own dreams would be fulfilled.

Their expectations of the Christ and His Kingdom would include national prosperity and freedom. They expected the Messiah to deliver Israel out of the bondage of the Roman Empire and establish David's throne in Jerusalem. They looked for an eternal righteous rule of God over all the earth. The world would embrace their faith, their belief, and their God. Of course, they also expected some personal perks. The disciples had often discussed, sometimes heatedly, their own places in the Kingdom. If Jesus is the Christ and if heaven has come down—if this is the time all have been waiting for—then there will be thrones and crowns and positions available for the faithful. And who was more faithful than the disciples?

THE GREAT INVITATION

But in contrast to all the disciples' expectations, Jesus began to speak of suffering and death. He would suffer at the hands of the chief priests. He would be rejected and killed. How could Jesus be the Christ and yet allow these things to happen? How could the disciples' plans come true if Jesus was not going to be with them?

Matthew's Gospel tells us that Peter began to rebuke Jesus: "Never, Lord! This shall never happen to you!" (Matthew 16:22). It was unthinkable that Jesus, now established as the Christ, would submit to His enemies and die rather than rout His enemies and reign over them. A divine Deliverer does not die. A divine Deliverer destroys enemies, establishes His rule, and offers spoils to His faithful.

Jesus invited His disciples to follow in His steps. They were interested in crowns, thrones, and spoils of victory, but Jesus invited them to deny themselves, to take up their cross and follow Him. Follow where? Follow to triumph and to heaven on earth? No, to follow in suffering, rejection, and death! When Jesus said "cross," He didn't have to draw them a picture. The Romans had been using this horrible method of execution on society's criminals for a long time. The disciples were celebrating their positions in the Kingdom, but Jesus invited them to self-denial and to degrading death.

What does the cross mean to us? The cross is more than a piece of jewelry, a symbol, or the memory of an event. The cross means death to our flesh, death to personal agenda, death to every hint of greed for personal gain. Everything the disciples expected—for Jesus and for themselves—had to go to the cross. Jesus still invites His people to follow in His own steps of self-denial and the cross. "What good is it for a man to gain the whole world, and yet lose or forfeit his very self?" (Luke 9:25).

THE GREAT REVELATION

Just a few days after these events, Jesus took Peter, James, and John up a mountain to pray. Here Jesus was transfigured before their eyes. "Two men, Moses and Elijah, appeared in glorious splendor, talking with Jesus. They spoke about his departure, which he was about to bring to fulfillment at Jerusalem" (Luke 9:30,31). I like that wording. Jesus was not talking with Moses and Elijah about things that would "happen" to Him, but about the things that He "was about to bring to fulfillment." Jesus' enemies were not in control; they never had been and never would be. Jesus was in charge. Jesus was orchestrating all of these events. He was never helpless, never at the mercy of anyone. He would bring it all to pass.

Again Peter spoke. He was wrong about building monuments to the experience but he was right when he said, "It is good for us to be here" (Luke 9:33). It was "good" for the disciples to see Moses and Elijah with Jesus in glory. It gave them assurance of Jesus' glory and further established Him as the Christ. They saw the glory that awaits the people of God.

The disciples had anticipated crowns, but were offered crosses. They wanted the Kingdom now, but Jesus was talking about the Kingdom later. They hoped for glory in this life, but Jesus was not offering that. They were confused and disappointed. It was "good" for them to catch this glimpse of glory, to see the real glory that would be theirs one day.

This vision of Jesus' glory and their future glory made an impact on these men. Peter later wrote that he was a witness of Christ's sufferings and was "one who also will share in the glory to be revealed" (1 Peter 5:1). John later wrote, "We have seen his glory" (John 1:14) and, "We shall be like him, for we shall see him as he is" (1 John 3:2). Growing close to the Lord teaches us that when God says no to one thing, He always says yes to something better.

THE GREAT TRANSFORMATION

Self-denial was not on the disciples' agenda and the cross was absolutely repulsive to them, but the Lord allowed three leaders of His group to see the end result of doing it His way. Glory. No earthly crown, no title, no throne, no honor or position can compare with the glory that is ours in Christ and that will be revealed. No suffering is too great a price to pay. "Now if we are children, then we are heirs—heirs of God and co-heirs with Christ, if indeed we share in his sufferings in order that we may also share in his glory. I consider that our present sufferings are not worth comparing with the glory that will be revealed in us" (Romans 8:17,18).

Have we had our own agendas? How much time and energy do we spend trying to have a pleasant and happy life, trying to be fulfilled and create our own heaven on earth? Does our reaction to disappointments and setbacks reflect an attitude of trust and hope of something better or does it reflect an attitude that says we need to get all we can now?

Recently I was reunited with a friend from college. I had not seen him for decades. My friend has cancer. Without a miracle, he hasn't much time left. No one has to tell him that heaven is not found on earth. I have a family member whose newborn child lived only a few hours. As I write this, the funeral is being arranged for this precious child. We don't have to explain to this young mother that heaven is not found on earth. What we hold on to is the hope of glory. "And we rejoice in the hope of the glory of God" (Romans 5:2). A few verses later we read that "hope does not disappoint us" (Romans 5:5).

No matter what happens, no matter the degree of suffering or the depth of disappointment we will endure, we have hope. We have a hope that will not disappoint us. Let's choose to live life with this assurance—whenever God says no to our expectations or goals, it is because He has something better. Let's accept the cross. Let's die to our own agendas, to our expectations and our own flesh so that we live for Christ and His glory alone. If we share in His sufferings, all the better. We will share in His glory.

Charles A. Davis graduated from North Central University in 1973 with a bachelor's degree in Bible and pastoral studies. He pastored in Bassett and Pender, Nebraska, before moving to Omaha. Since 1988 he has served as senior pastor at South Side Assembly of God in Omaha (southsideassembly.com).

Davis serves as a sectional presbyter in the Nebraska District Council, on the board of directors for Teen Challenge of the Midlands and as an NCU alumni representative for Nebraska.

Charles and Yvonne Davis have three children. Bryan and Laura Davis are missionaries in Senegal, West Africa (davisinsenegal.org). Derrick and Courtney Davis serve as youth pastors at South Side Assembly of God (ventureyouth.com). David and Alissa (Davis) Scrabeck are recent graduates from NCU.

CHAPTER 25

Fixing a Broken Prayer Life

KEN HORN

Prayer. It is the Christian's lifeline to Jesus. It is the highest privilege granted the believer. The Bible is filled with promises that God will respond to sincere prayer.

Yet, too often, it seems as if it just doesn't work. Answers don't come, circumstances don't change, and God's people wander in a state of perpetual confusion—discouraged by this seeming lack of concern on the Lord's part and too embarrassed by it to share their feelings with others.

So what's the deal? Why does it seem prayer doesn't work for many of us the way it works for others? Is there something I could be doing, or not doing, that is short-circuiting my prayer life?

There are indeed a number of things that become barriers to an effective prayer life. They fit into three categories: things that keep us from *praying*; things that keep us from *getting answers*; and things that keep us from *recognizing answers*. Let's look at the possible problems and the ways to fix them.

THINGS THAT KEEP US FROM PRAYING

Prayer can't work if believers don't do it. "You do not have because you do not ask" (James 4:2, NKJV). There are several things that keep our prayer lives short . . . or nonexistent.

Love for the things of the world

Many Christians give massive amounts of time to pursue worldly things. Love for these things drives people to spend more time with them than with the things of God, and even to think about these things while in God's house. Love for the things of the world inevitably leads to indifference to the things of God.

Indifference, or lukewarmness, will make prayer seem like wasted time, or drive it from our minds completely. The Bible says the person who prays little and is not convicted about it is distasteful to God (see Revelation 3:16). The spiritually lazy person finds little joy in serving Jesus.

Genuine delight in the Lord is a key to answered prayer. "Delight yourself also in the Lord, and He shall give you the desires of your heart" (Psalm 37:4).

Substitution . . . with good things

Many Christians have a "spiritual sweet tooth," in the words of St. John of the Cross, a 16th-century Christian. By this he meant that many believers spend more time reading about or listening about serving God than actually doing it.

I love to read books on prayer. But when books on prayer outweigh one's prayer life, something needs to change. One can read too many Christian books, listen to too many sermons, and watch too much Christian television . . . *if* those things have become a substitute for actually spending time with God. We must not be content to live off the experiences of others.

Andrew Bonar had an unusual definition of fasting—abstaining from anything that hinders prayer. Bonar, an avid reader, recognized that even his love for Christian books could take God's time. He periodically fasted from reading to pursue God more personally.

Misplaced priorities

Lots of people don't pray because they feel they just don't have the time. Martin Luther, the great reformer, said, "I am so busy that if I did not spend two or three hours each day in prayer I could not get through the day." While this amount of prayer is probably unrealistic for most Christians, 10 minutes or 15 minutes isn't. Yet believers appeal to their busy schedules as reasons for not giving even this small amount of time to God.

People find time for things that are important to them. Make prayer a priority and you will pray more.

Distractions

Prayer is a magnet. Just as soon as we determine to pray, every distraction imaginable is attracted to us. Call it "distraction attraction." The phone rings, someone enters the room, or, most commonly, our mind wanders. We think of something else we need (or want) to do and our time with God is either shortened or diluted.

When Satan sees your prayer life beginning to grow, he wants to do anything he can to distract you from it. Fight distraction by minimizing what you can externally and asking for God's help in dealing with the internal ones.

Reluctance to pray with others

Many Christians routinely miss opportunities to strengthen their prayer life by praying with others.

Consider the power of united prayer, as described by Jesus: "Again I say to you that if two of you agree on earth concerning anything that they ask, it will be done for them by My Father in heaven. For where two or three are gathered together in My name, I am there in the midst of them" (Matthew 18:19,20).

Make an effort to pray with others.

A perceived lack of credibility

What keeps couples from praying together?

Often it is because one or both of the spouses feel that, since their spouse knows what they are really like (and that may not appear very spiritual), they lack credibility to pray at home. But that just makes prayer together all the more important.

Contra many, I don't believe you need to be exactly the same (outwardly) at home as you are in church. Corporate worship is different from private or family worship. Certainly, you must not be a hypocrite, but it is all right to develop a unique prayer and worship style at home that is suitable to your family.

THINGS THAT KEEP US FROM GETTING ANSWERS

The Bible has clearly listed several of these.

Unconfessed sin

"One sin allowed in a life wrecks our usefulness, stifles our joy, and robs prayer of its power." So said Dick Eastman in his book *No Easy Road*.

Scripture agrees. Psalm 66:18 (KJV) addresses this when the psalmist says, "If I regard iniquity in my heart, the Lord will not hear me." Sound harsh?

Many fear that there is some sin that they have forgotten to specifically mention that God will forever hold over their head. But the verse doesn't say that. The word "regard," the Hebrew *raah*, means to "see" or "look at" by direct volition. It is a sin of which one is aware.

"The Lord looks at the heart" (1 Samuel 16:7, NKJV). Jesus "had no need that anyone should testify of man, for He knew what was in man" (John 2:25). When a person prays while holding on to a cherished sin, God always knows . . . and tragically, He turns a deaf ear.

Eventually, as Leonard Ravenhill has said, "A sinning man

will stop praying, and a praying man will stop sinning."

First John 1:9 has the solution: "If we confess our sins, He is faithful and just to forgive us our sins and to cleanse us from all unrighteousness." Psalm 119:11 has the long-term solution: "Your word I have hidden in my heart, that I might not sin against You."

A poor husband-wife relationship

First Peter 3:7 says, "Husbands, likewise, dwell with them with understanding, giving honor to the wife, as to the weaker vessel, and as being heirs together of the grace of life, that your prayers may not be hindered." When a husband and wife are not getting along, their prayers are hindered. Ephesians 4:26 says, "Do not let the sun go down while you are still angry" (NIV).

Florence and Percy Arrowsmith broke a world record when they celebrated their 80th wedding anniversary in 2005. Florence, 100, told the BBC that their secret was, you must "never be afraid to say 'sorry'" and "You must never go to sleep bad friends." (Percy, 105, said his secret to marital bliss was two words: "Yes, dear.")

One of the reasons many homes have no family devotional time is that it's difficult to feel spiritual if you've been arguing or are upset at one another. But rather than letting this keep spouses from praying, a determination to pray together daily would keep problems from festering.

The old saying is true: "The family that prays together stays together."

An unforgiving spirit

I sat with an unsaved man in a hospital waiting room as his wife, a member of my church, was having major surgery. His heart was tender and he was open to the gospel. "Tony" was ready to commit his life to Jesus. But first, he said, he had one question. "Do I have to forgive everyone to become a Christian?" he asked.

"Yes," I said, sharing some Scriptures with him.

"Then I can't be a Christian," he told me. "There are some people I can't forgive. I'll have to go to hell."

I have never had more tragic words said to me. But unforgiveness can also creep into Christian lives.

One of Jesus' classic statements on prayer is directly followed by instruction on the importance of forgiveness. "And whenever you stand praying, if you have anything against anyone, forgive him, that your Father in heaven may also forgive you your trespasses. But if you do not forgive, neither will your Father in heaven forgive your trespasses" (Mark 11:25,26, NKJV).

Unforgiveness becomes a barrier to answered prayer. If you have unforgiveness in your heart, drop everything and make it right. (See Matthew 5:23,24.)

A proud spirit

Luke 18:10-14 recounts the story of two men. One was a Pharisee who prayed, "God, I thank You that I am not like other men—extortioners, unjust, adulterers, or even as this tax collector" (v. 11). The other, a tax collector, cried with his head down, "God, be merciful to me a sinner!" (v. 13).

"I tell you," Jesus said in verse 14, "this man went down to his house justified rather than the other; for everyone who exalts himself will be humbled, and he who humbles himself will be exalted."

Proud prayers are worse than no prayers. It seems that people who are not proud in any other way can be condescending spiritually.

"Therefore humble yourselves under the mighty hand of God, that He may exalt you in due time," 1 Peter 5:6 enjoins. Humility eventually is rewarded. But remember God's *due time* for answered prayer. It matters not who we are. "He shall regard the prayer of the destitute, and shall not despise their prayer" (Psalm 102:17).

Doubt

"Whatever things you ask when you pray, believe that you receive them, and you will have them" (Mark 11:24). Doubt and faith cannot coexist, according to James 1:6-8.

But only a little faith is required. The first three Gospels record a time when the disciples could not cast a demon out of a man's son (Matthew 17:14-21; Mark 9:17-29; Luke 9:38-43). They were called "faithless" because they had given up (Matthew 17:17). It was a difficult case and they had no permanent stake in it. On the other hand, the father couldn't give up; it was his son.

The disciples didn't even have mustard-seed size faith (Matthew 17:20). But the father did. Still he cried, "Lord, I believe; help my unbelief!" (Mark 9:24). It was enough, and Jesus answered by delivering his son.

What you may think is doubt or unbelief may simply be little faith. A mustard seed is very small. Don't count little faith as unbelief. You don't need great faith—just a little faith in a great God. The small step of faith tests the bridge, but the strength of the bridge gets the traveler across.

Lack of intensity

After chiding the disciples for unbelief, Jesus added, "However, this kind [of demon] does not go out except by prayer and fasting" (Matthew 17:21). James 5:16 says, "The effective, fervent prayer of a righteous man avails much." God is looking for serious prayer, and some cases require spiritual warfare, which sometimes includes fasting.

Weymouth translates the verse this way: "The heartfelt supplication of a righteous man exerts a mighty influence." God wants you to put your heart into your prayer.

Lack of time in the Scriptures

Prayer and the Word are two sides of the same spiritual coin. They must go together. Time in God's Word makes for a healthy Christian walk and an enhanced prayer life. Ignoring God's Word negatively impacts the prayer life.

The extreme: "One who turns away his ear from hearing the law, even his prayer is an abomination" (Proverbs 28:9).

The promise: "This Book of the Law shall not depart from your mouth, but you shall meditate in it day and night, that you may observe to do according to all that is written in it. For then you will make your way prosperous, and then you will have good success" (Joshua 1:8).

THINGS THAT KEEP US FROM RECOGNIZING ANSWERS

Earlier I noted that many question, "Why doesn't prayer work for many of us the way it works for others?" We are certainly more likely to notice the dramatic answers. But even so-called spiritual giants wrestle with answers they don't like. I have heard it said that God answers prayer in four ways: (1) "No, not yet"; (2) "No, I love you too much"; (3) "Yes, I thought you'd never ask"; and (4) "Yes, and here's more."

Asking amiss

James 4:3 says, "You ask and do not receive, because you ask amiss, that you may spend it on your pleasures." When people pray from improper motives, or for things that God knows would be detrimental to them, the answer is likely to be "No."

Expecting amiss

Be prepared for God to answer contrary to your wishes. Three times Paul asked for his thorn in the flesh to be removed.

But God's response was, "My grace is sufficient for you, for My strength is made perfect in weakness" (2 Corinthians 12:9). Paul's prayer wasn't selfish; but it was contrary to a lesson God wanted Paul to learn.

The answer is found in James 4:15: "Instead you ought to say, 'If the Lord wills, we shall live and do this or that.' " Seek the Lord's will first. When you have a strong sense of His will in your life you can pray with confidence.

WHAT YOU CAN DO

Take an inventory of your prayer life, using the hindrances listed above. With God's help, correct those areas that need work.

Pray in the authority of Christ's name, which can only be done if you are praying according to His will. "And whatever you ask in My name, that I will do, that the Father may be glorified in the Son. If you ask anything in My name, I will do it" (John 14:13,14).

Most of all, get wrapped up in Jesus. John 15:7 summarizes what that means to one's prayer life: "If you abide in Me, and My words abide in you, you will ask what you desire, and it shall be done for you."

For the author's biographical information, see "About the Editors" on page 238.

ENDNOTES

Chapter 8

1. *Daily Telegram*, Adrian, Michigan, July 2005.
2. Spiros Zodhiates, editor, *Hebrew Greek Key Study Bible*.
3. Smith Wigglesworth, *Apostle of Faith*, 135.

Chapter 10

1. Michael Hill, Associated Press, November 2, 2005.

Chapter 12

1. "Revival in Belfast," Robin Mark, Hosanna Music.

2. *Strong's Hebrew and Chaldee Dictionary of the Old Testament* #7303.

3. "I wish that all the Lord's people were prophets and that the Lord would put his Spirit on them!" (Numbers 11:29, all NIV unless otherwise noted).

4. *Strong's Greek Dictionary of the New Testament* #3875.

5. "And these signs shall follow them that believe; In my name shall they cast out devils; they shall speak with new tongues" (Mark 16:17, KJV).

6. "The wind blows wherever it pleases. You hear its sound, but you cannot tell where it comes from or where it is going. So it is with everyone born of the Spirit" (John 3:8).

7. "He saved us through the washing of rebirth and renewal by the Holy Spirit" (Titus 3:5).

8. "But you were washed, you were sanctified, you were justified in the name of the Lord Jesus Christ and by the Spirit of our God" (1 Corinthians 6:11).

9. "Suddenly a sound like the blowing of a violent wind came from heaven and filled the whole house where they were sitting. They saw what seemed to be tongues of fire that separated and came to rest on each of them. All of them were filled with the Holy Spirit and began to speak in other tongues as the Spirit enabled them" (Acts 2:2-4).

10. "Peter replied, 'Repent and be baptized, every one of you, in the name of Jesus Christ for the forgiveness of your sins. And you will receive the gift of the Holy Spirit. The promise is for you and your children and for all who are far off—for all whom the Lord our God will call'" (Acts 2:38,39).

11. "And hope does not disappoint us, because God has poured out his love into our hearts by the Holy Spirit, whom he has given us" (Romans 5:5).

12. "For they heard them speaking in tongues and praising God" (Acts 10:46).

Chapter 13

1. Roy Lessin, *God's Heart to Yours!* (Honor Books).

Chapter 14

1. Do not resuscitate.

Chapter 22

1. Stephen R. Covey, *The 7 Habits of Highly Effective People* (New York: Simon and Schuster, 1989), 235.

Chapter 23

1. Copied, source unknown.

NOTES

ABOUT THE EDITORS

George O. Wood *is the general secretary of the Assemblies of God. The son of missionary parents to China and Tibet, he holds a doctoral degree in pastoral theology from Fuller Theological Seminary, a juris doctorate from Western State University College of Law, and membership in the California State Bar. He is the author of several books, including* A Psalm in Your Heart *(2 volumes) and a college text on the Book of* Acts.

Dr. Wood formerly served as assistant superintendent for the Southern California District of the Assemblies of God and pastored 17 years at Newport-Mesa Christian Life Center in Costa Mesa, California. Dr. Wood and his wife, Jewel, have two children, Evangeline and George Paul.

Hal Donaldson *is editor in chief of* Today's Pentecostal Evangel, *the official voice of the Assemblies of God and the world's largest Pentecostal magazine. Donaldson also serves as founder and president of Convoy of Hope, a nonprofit ministry that conducts humanitarian/evangelism efforts across America and around the world. Through Convoy of Hope, millions of needy families have received groceries, Bibles, medical attention, and job opportunities. And many have accepted Jesus Christ as Savior and been assimilated into local churches.*

Donaldson is the author of some 20 books, including: Midnight in the City, One Man's Compassion *(the Mark Buntain story),* Treasures in Heaven *(the Huldah Buntain story),* The Vow, Pleasing God, Where is the Lost Ark?, Parenting, *and more. A graduate of Bethany University of the Assemblies of God, where he served as an instructor, Donaldson also has a B.A. in journalism from San Jose State University. He and his wife, Doree, have four daughters: Lindsay, Erin-Rae, Lauren, and Haly.*

Ken Horn is managing editor of Today's Pentecostal Evangel. *He received his bachelor's degree from Bethany University, an M.A. from Simpson College, the D.Min. from California Graduate School of Theology, and did additional graduate work at Golden Gate Theological Seminary. Horn pastored three churches in California and Oregon. He has taught theology and related subjects on the graduate and undergraduate levels at Assemblies of God Theological Seminary, Simpson College and other institutions. His published books include* Revival Sermons, Living Like Jesus, *and* Silk Road Stories. *He and his wife, Peggy, traveled as missionary evangelists in Eastern Europe in the 1980s.*

Wood, Donaldson and Horn collaborated on a previous book, *Trusting God: Answers for Troubled Times,* also available from Onward Books, Inc.

For a complete list
of books
offered by
Onward Books, Inc.
please call or write:

Onward Books, Inc.
4848 South Landon Court
Springfield, MO 65810
417-890-7465

Or visit our
Web site at:
www.onwardbooks.com